mel bay's full-page chord diagram book

tear-out sheets

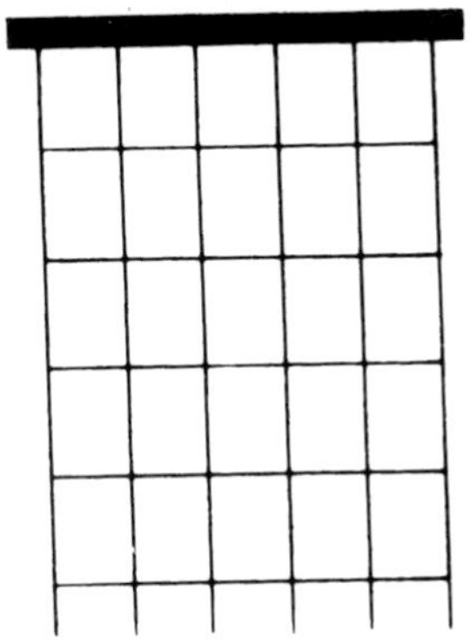
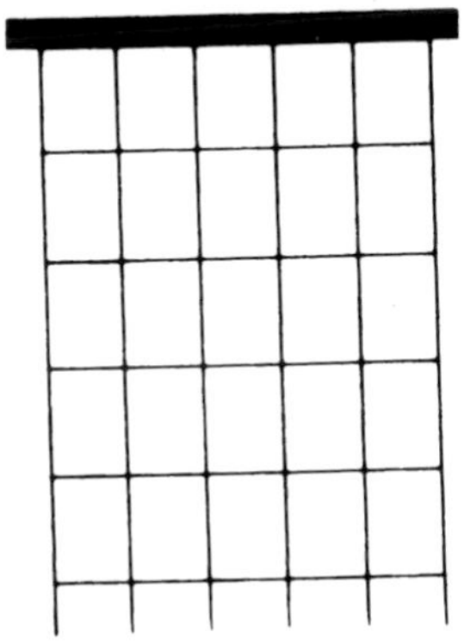
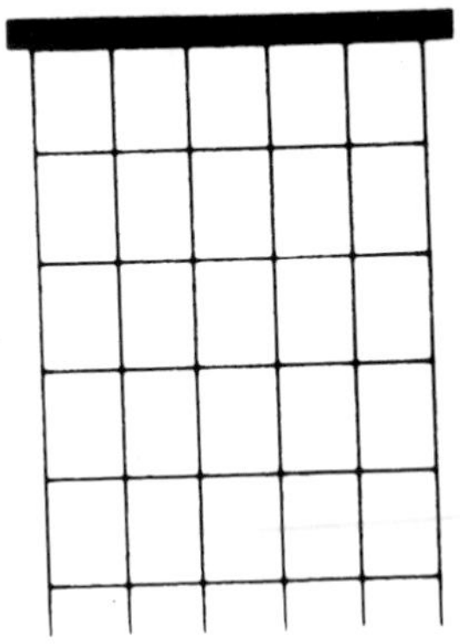
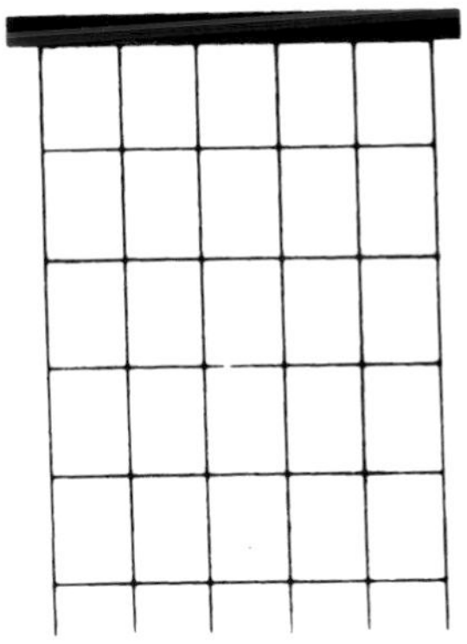
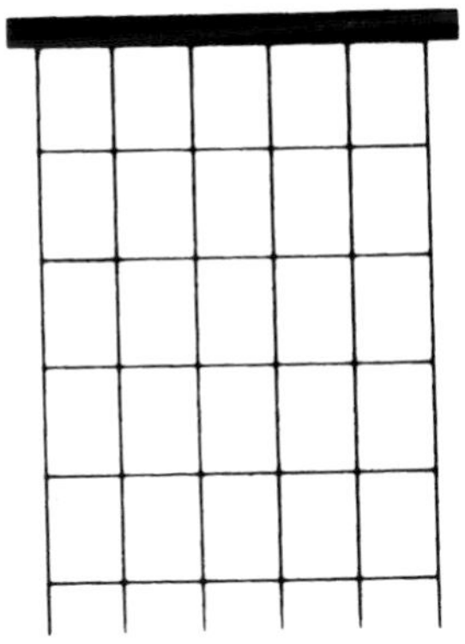

MEL BAY

GUITAR CHORDS

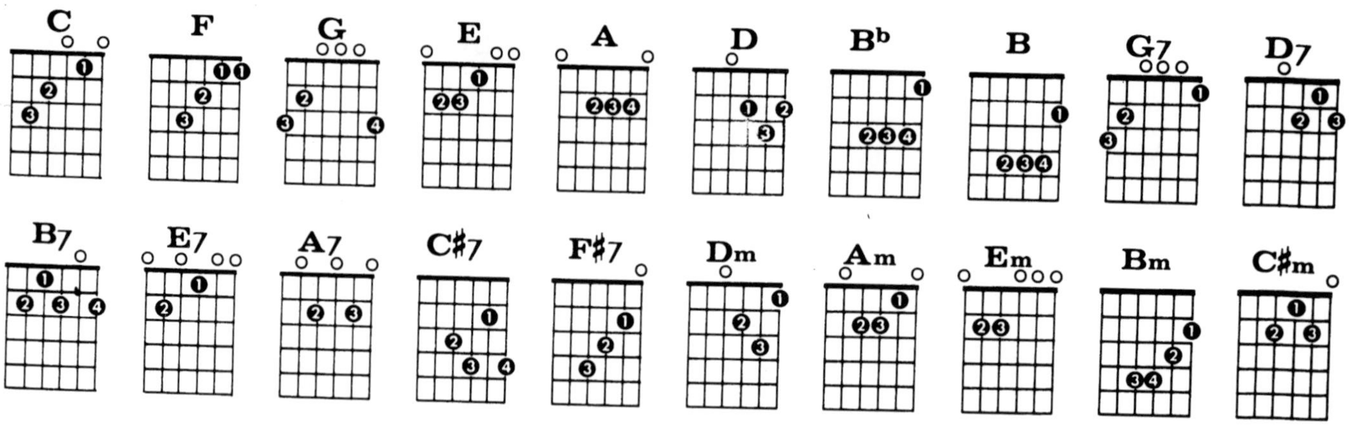

TENOR BANJO CHORDS

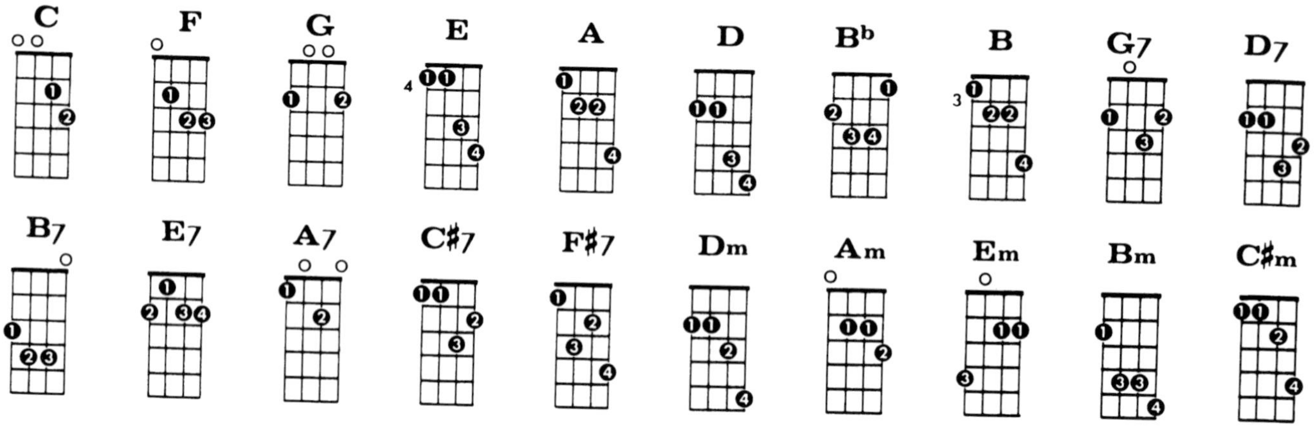

BANJO CHORDS (Bluegrass G Tuning)

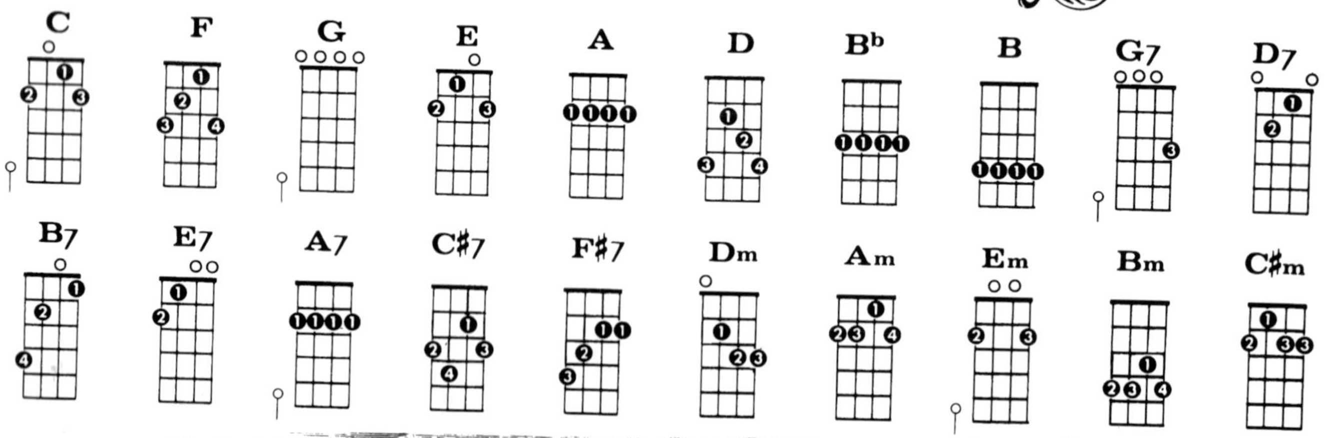

UKULELE CHORDS (C Tuning: G,C,E,A)

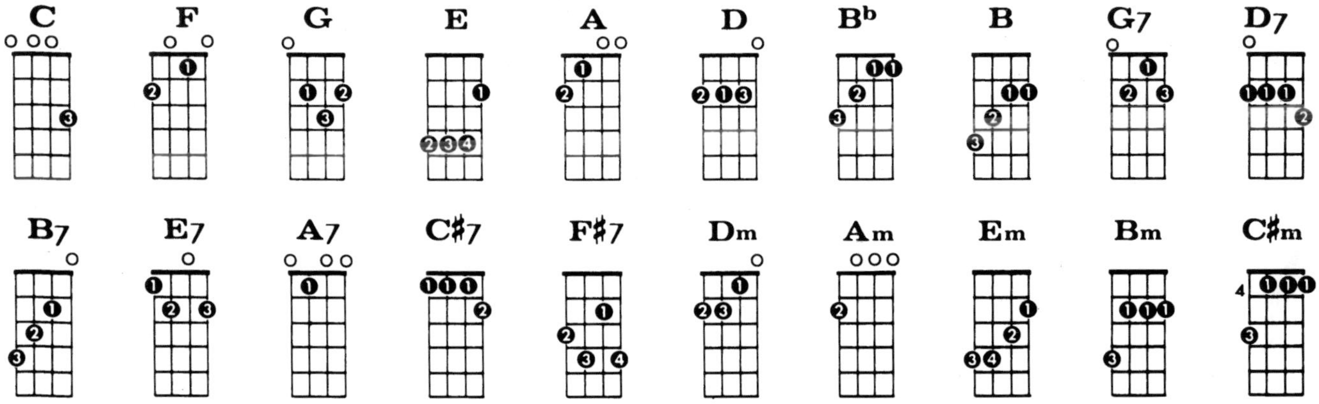

BARITONE UKE CHORDS (Tuning: E,B,G,D)

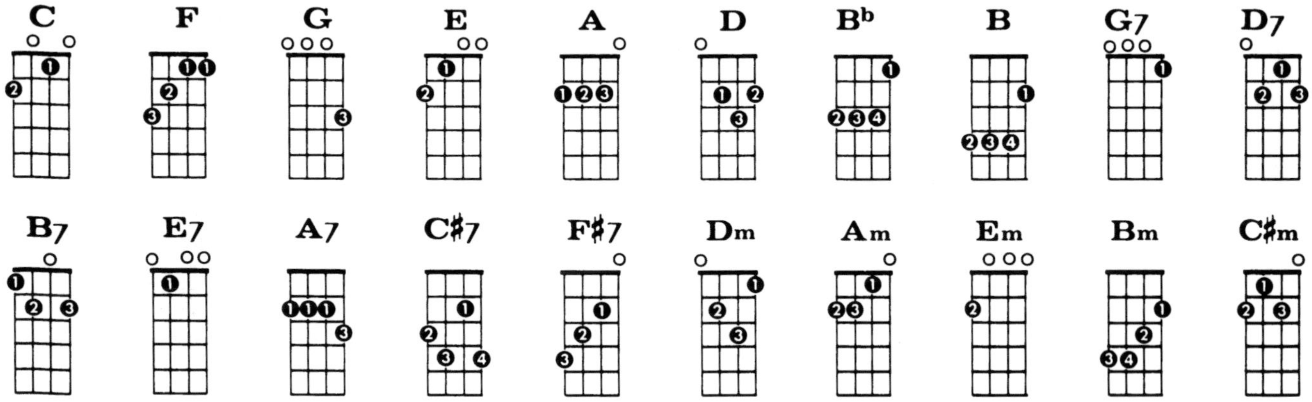

MANDOLIN CHORDS

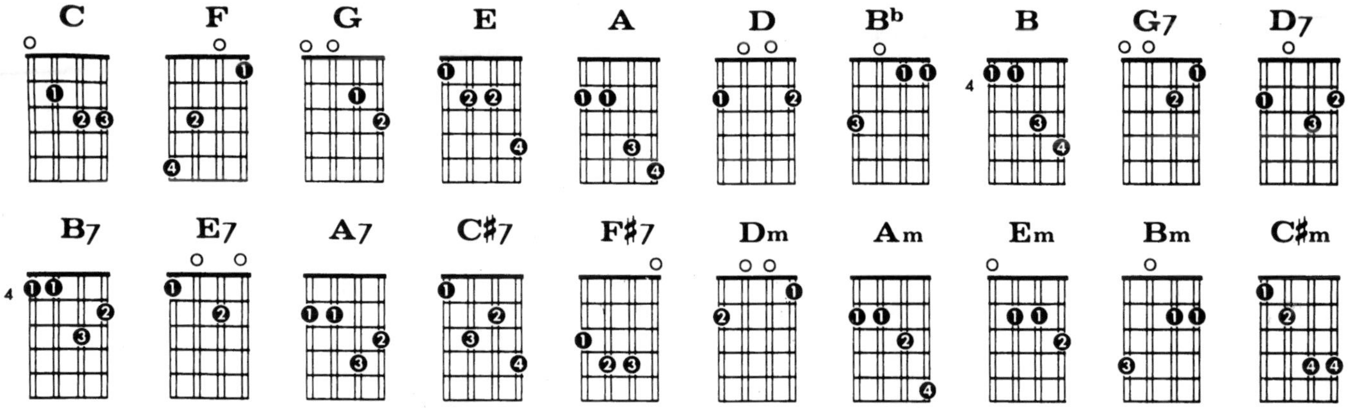

EXPLANATION OF CHORD SYMBOLS

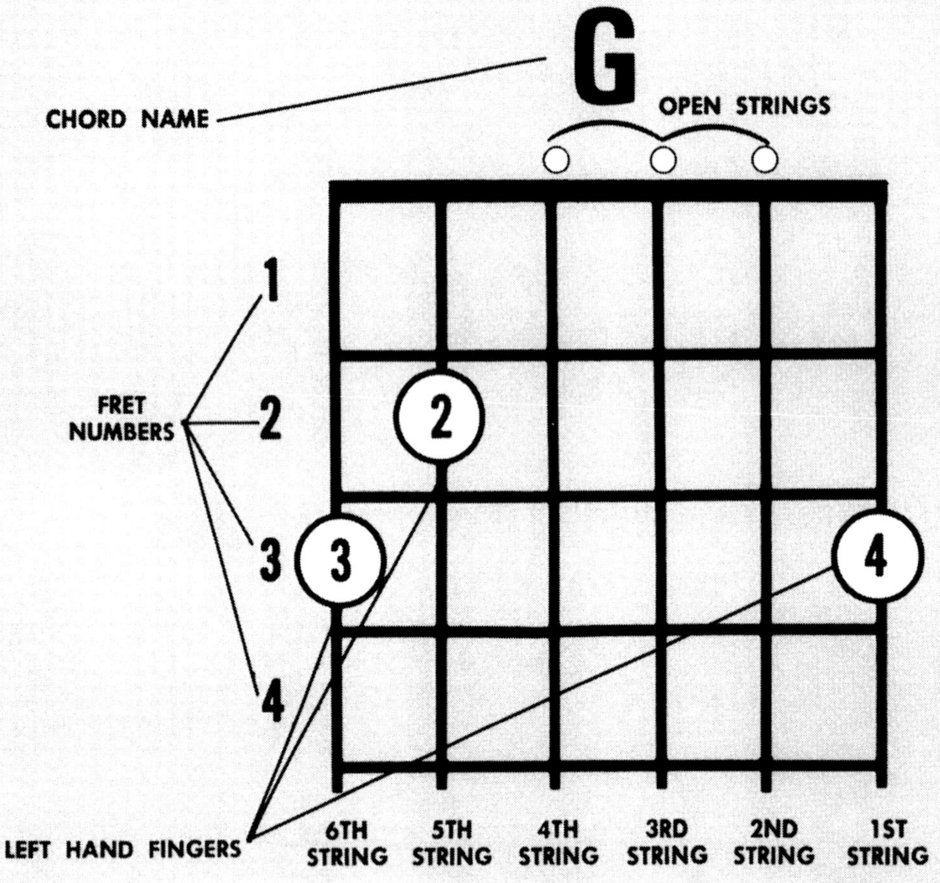

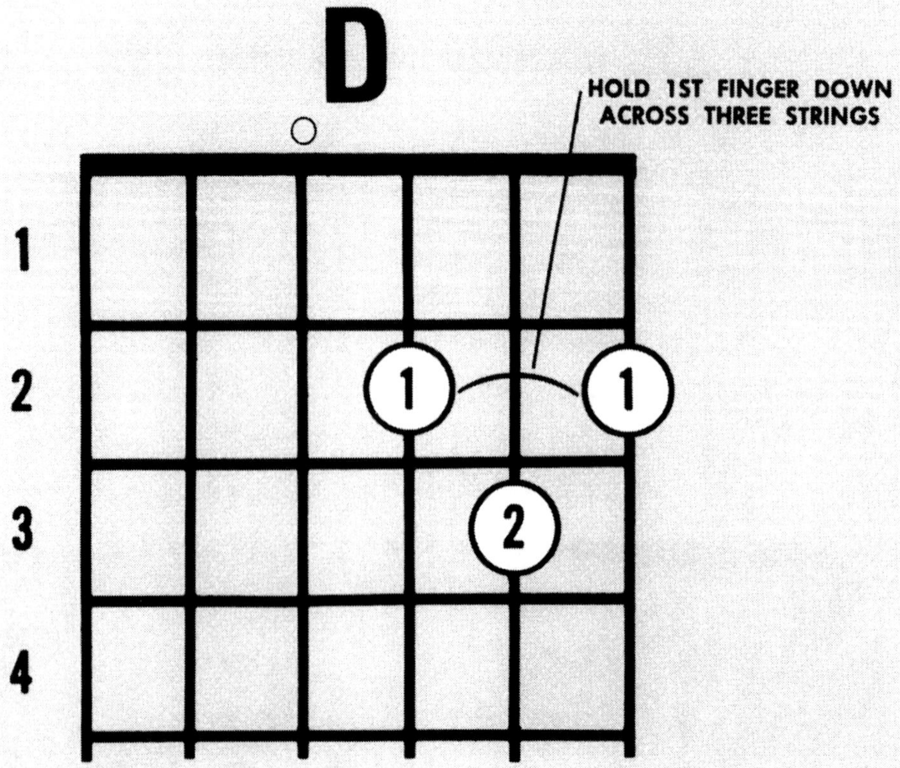

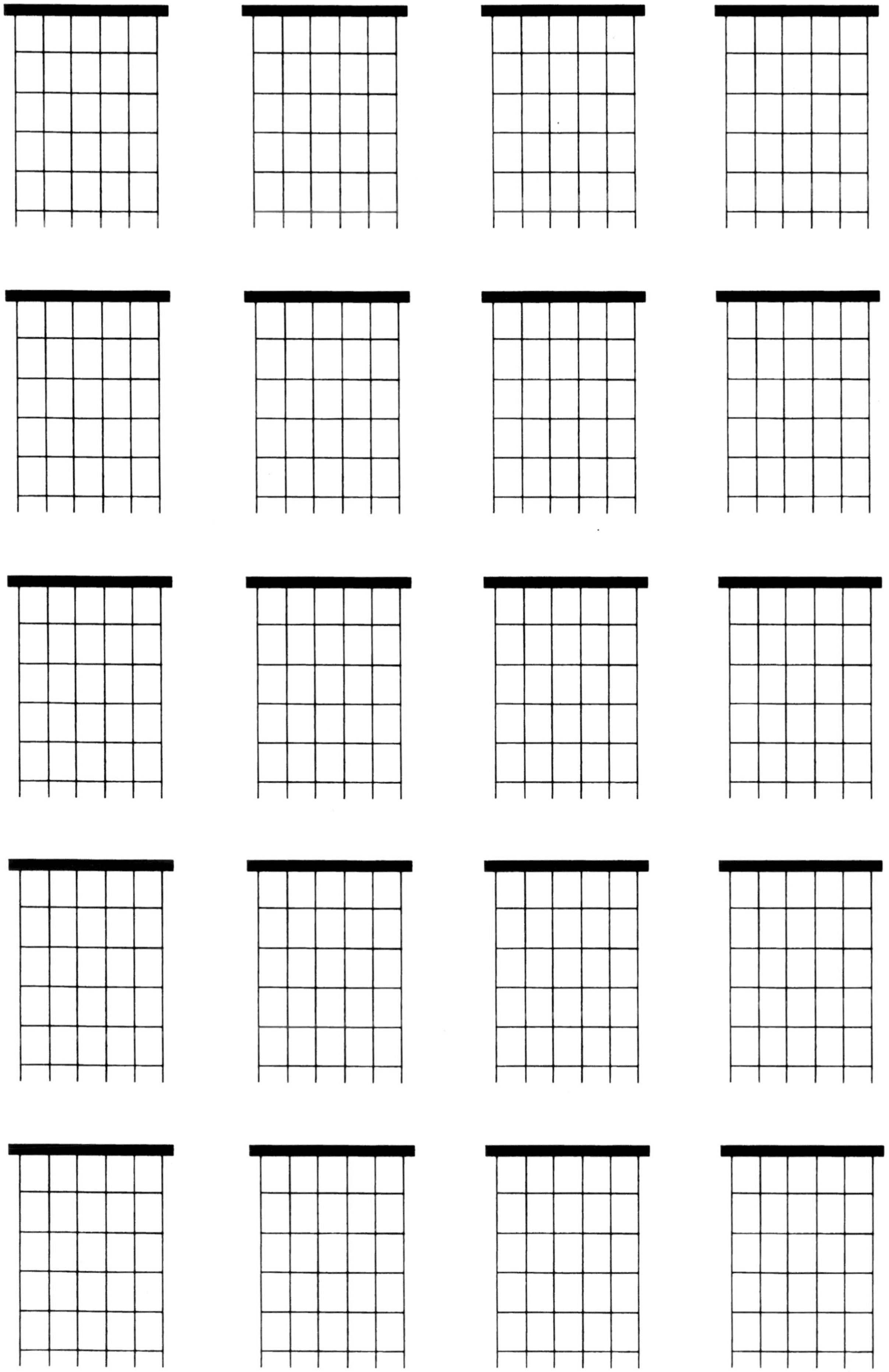

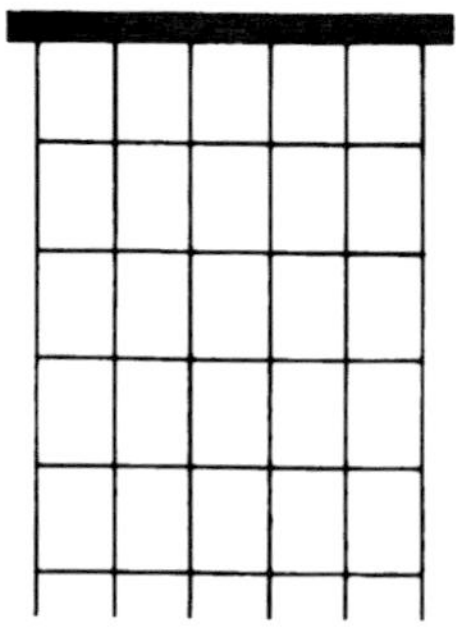 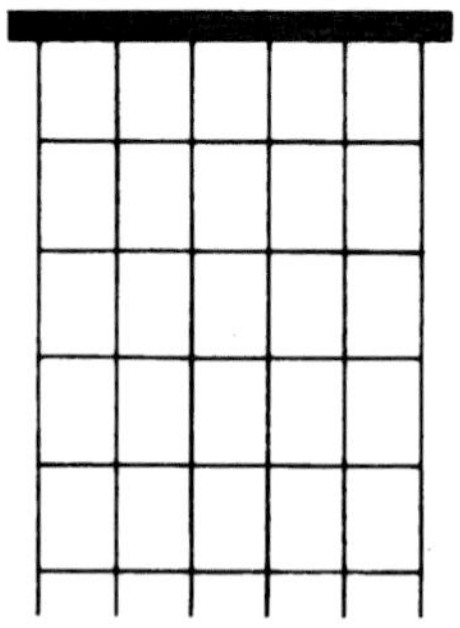 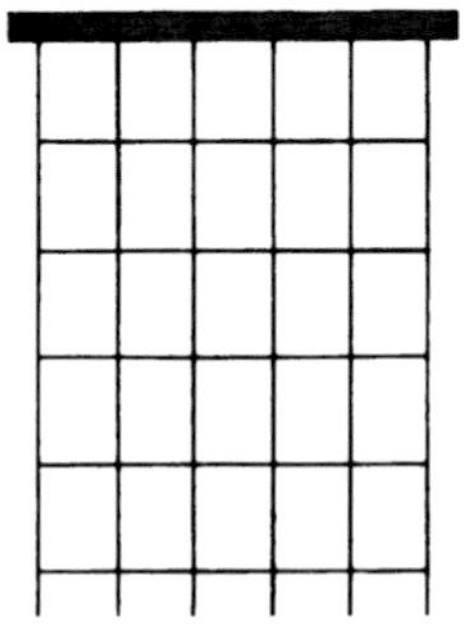 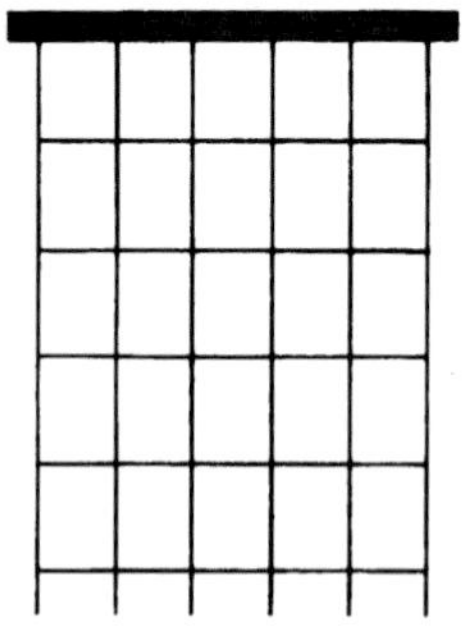

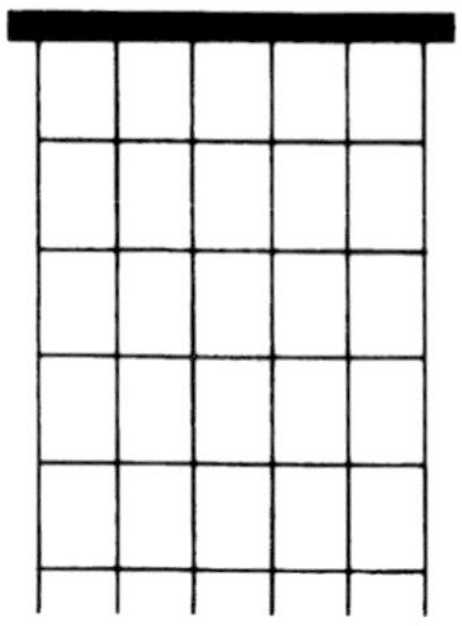 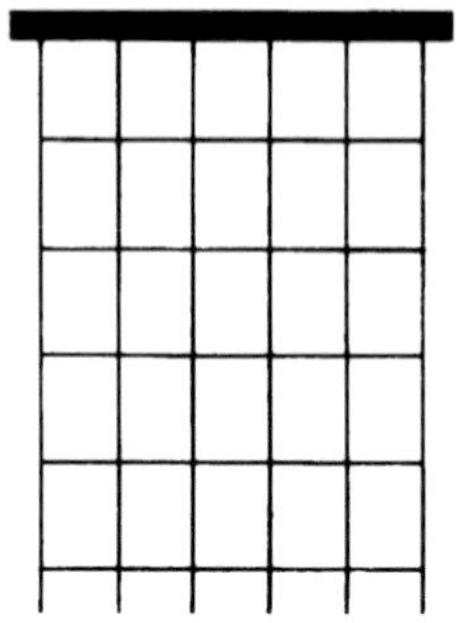 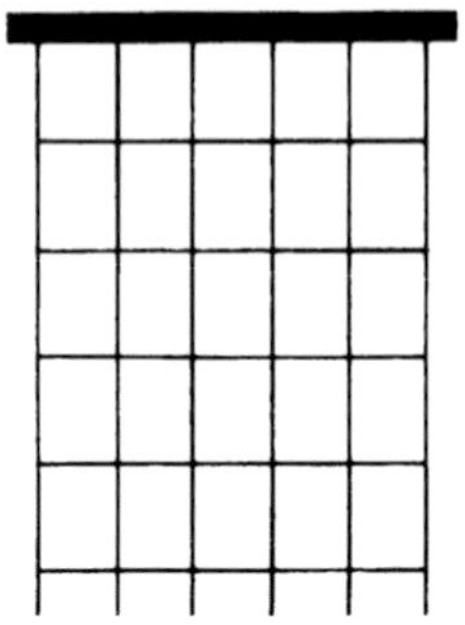 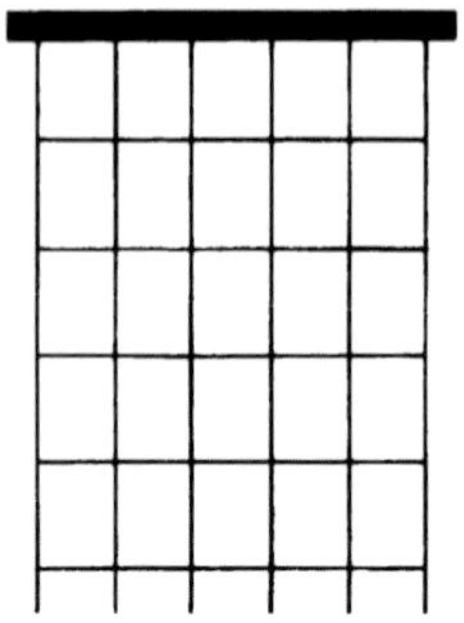

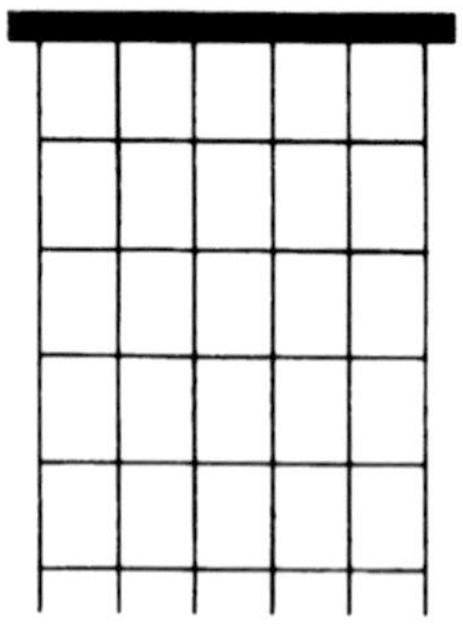 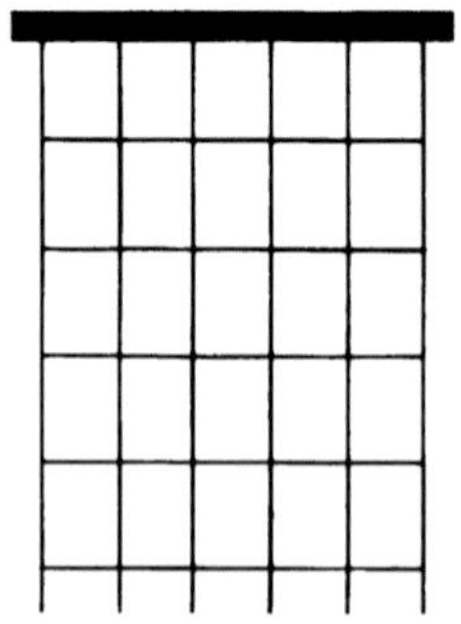 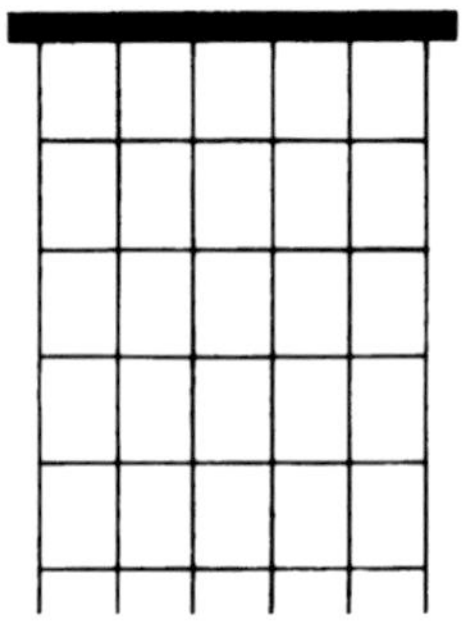 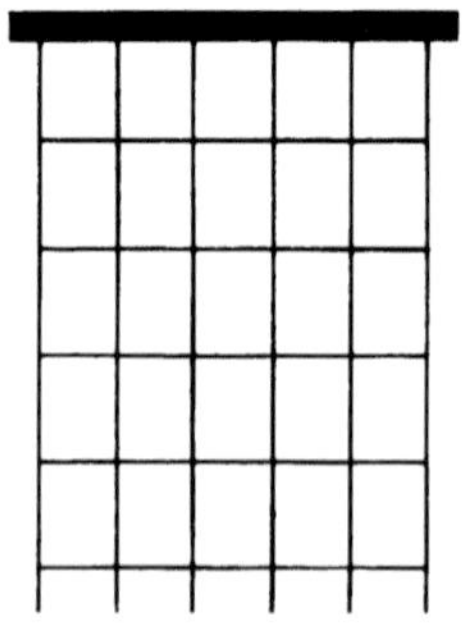

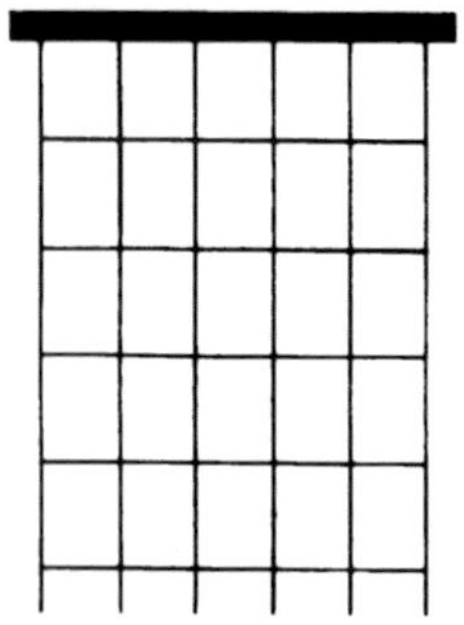 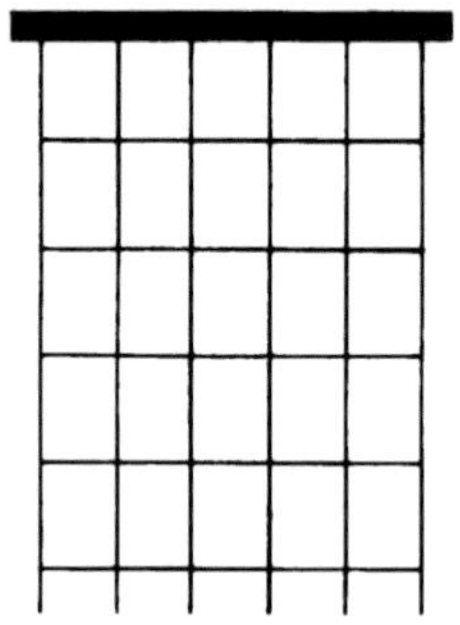 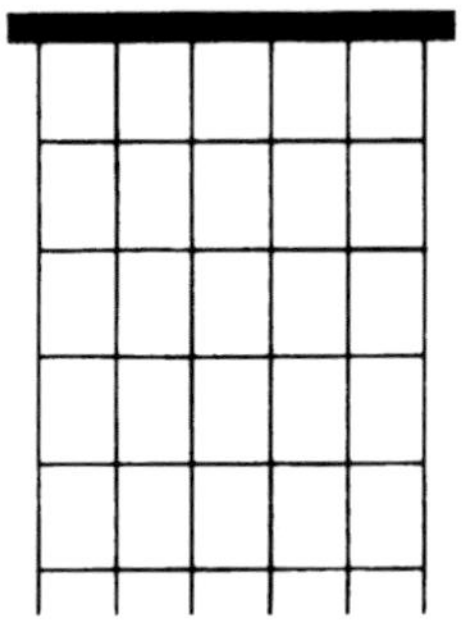 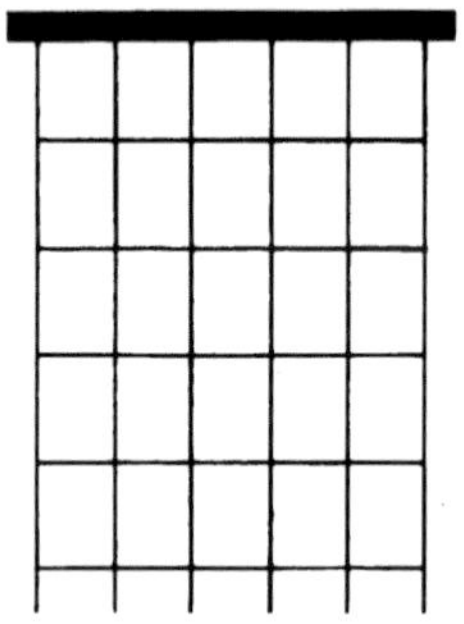

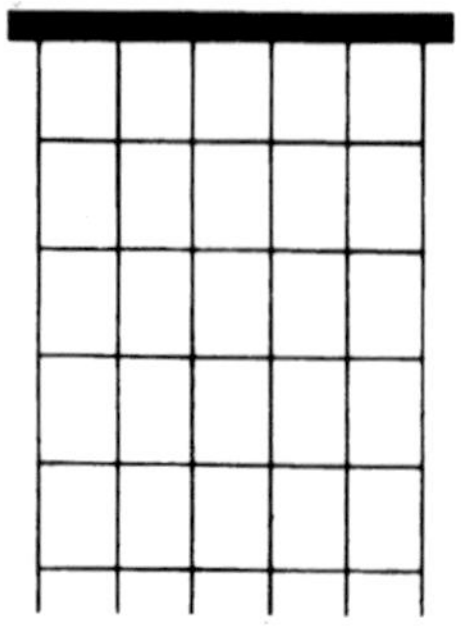 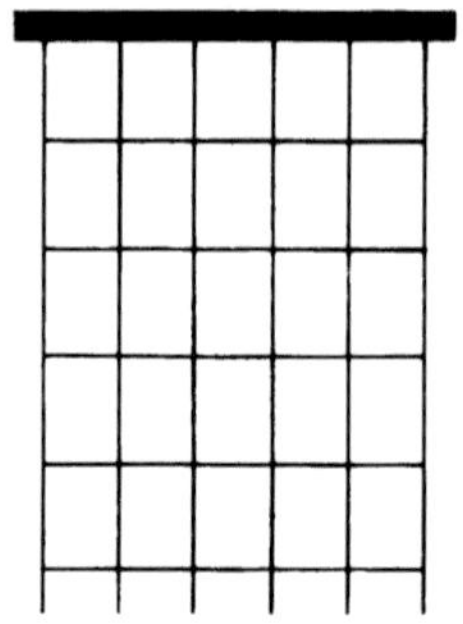 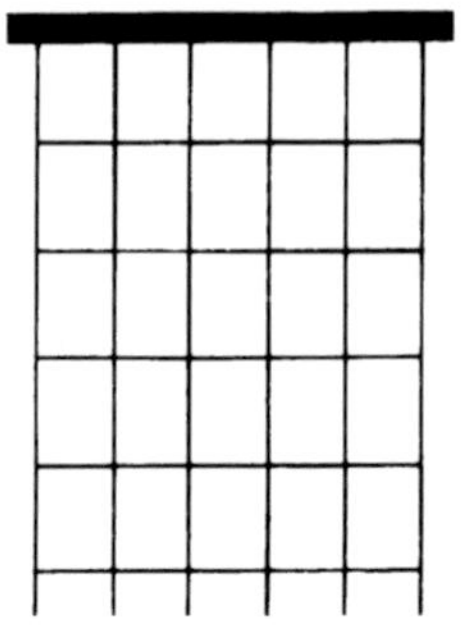 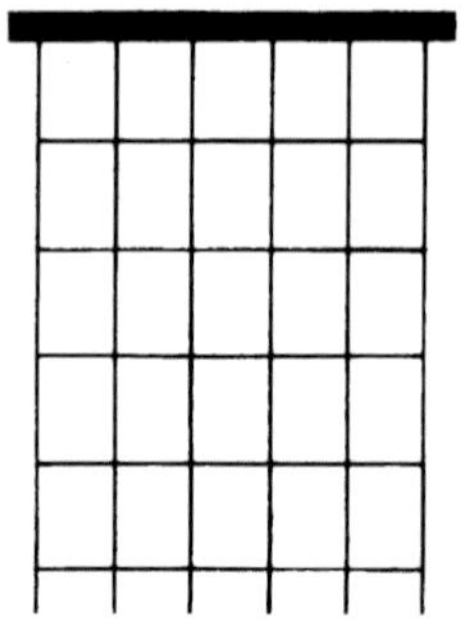

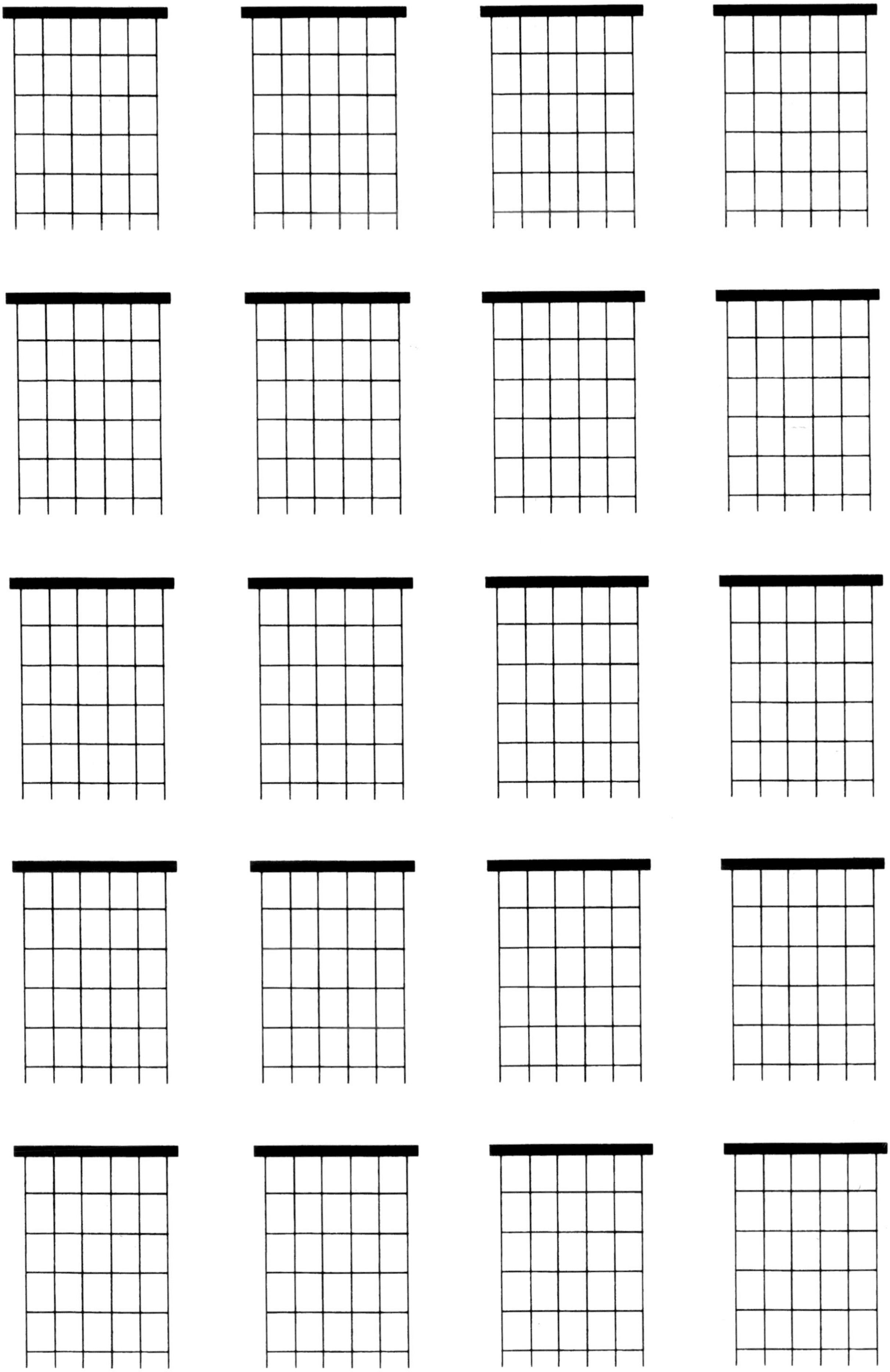

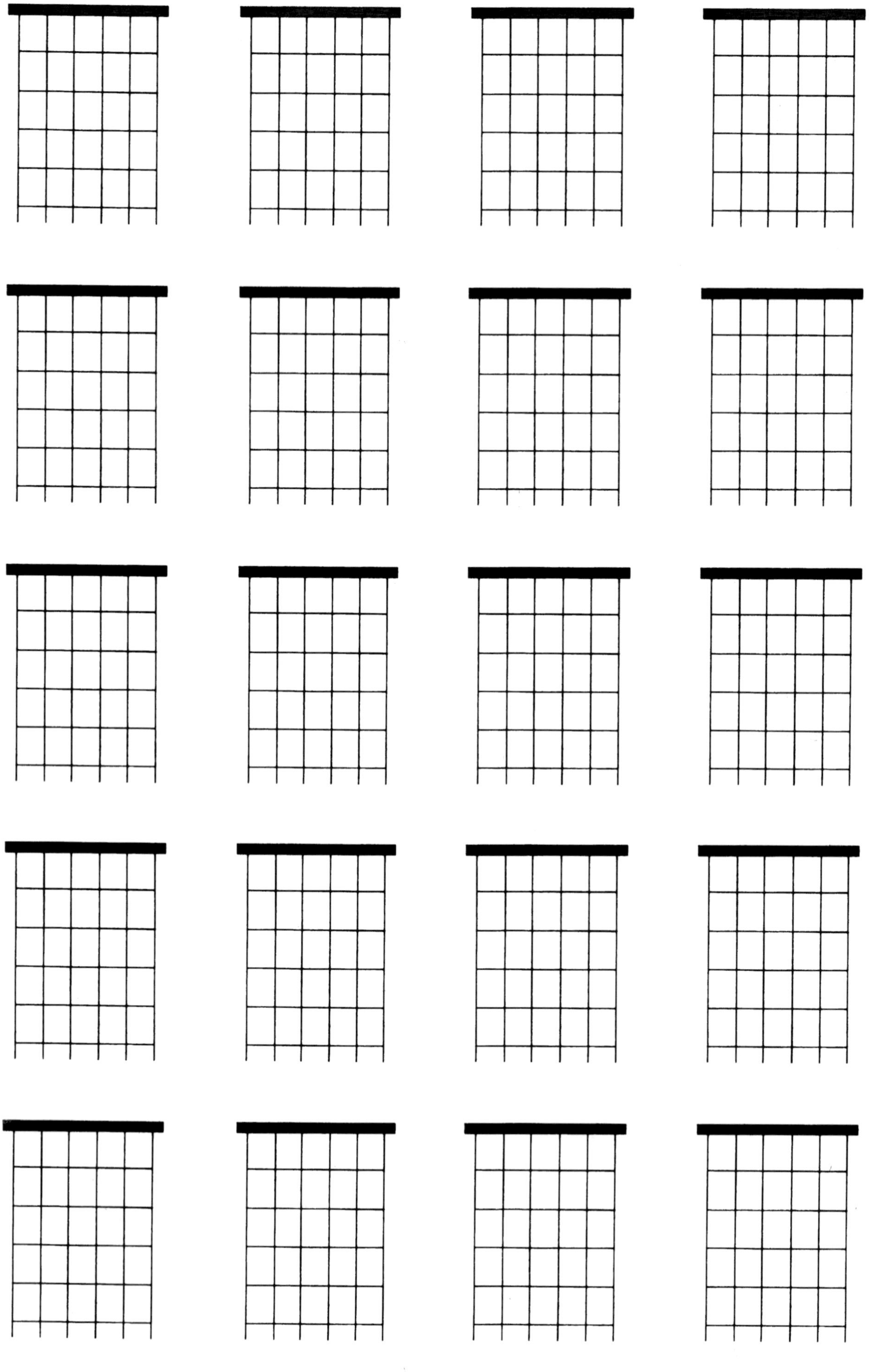

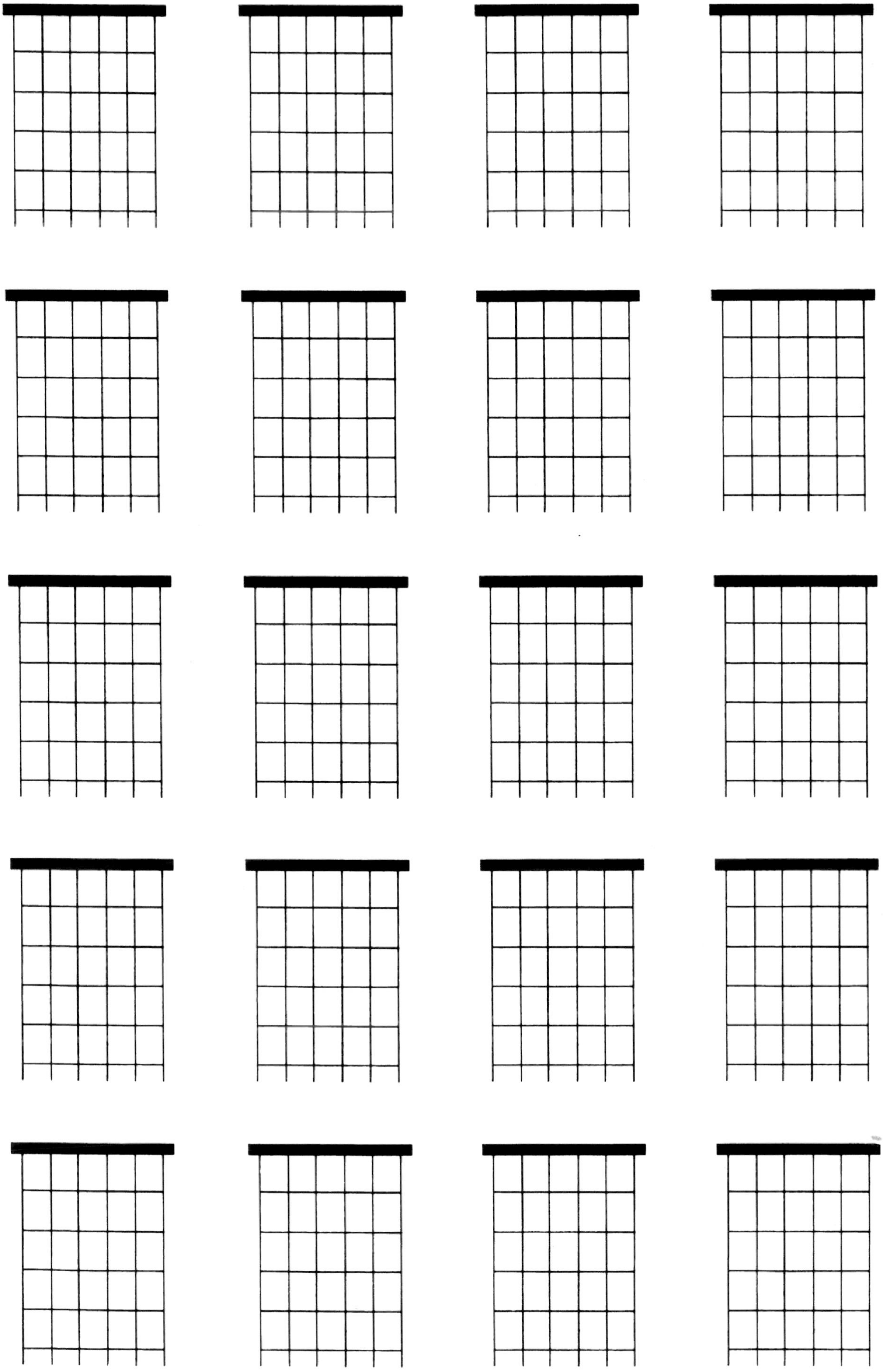

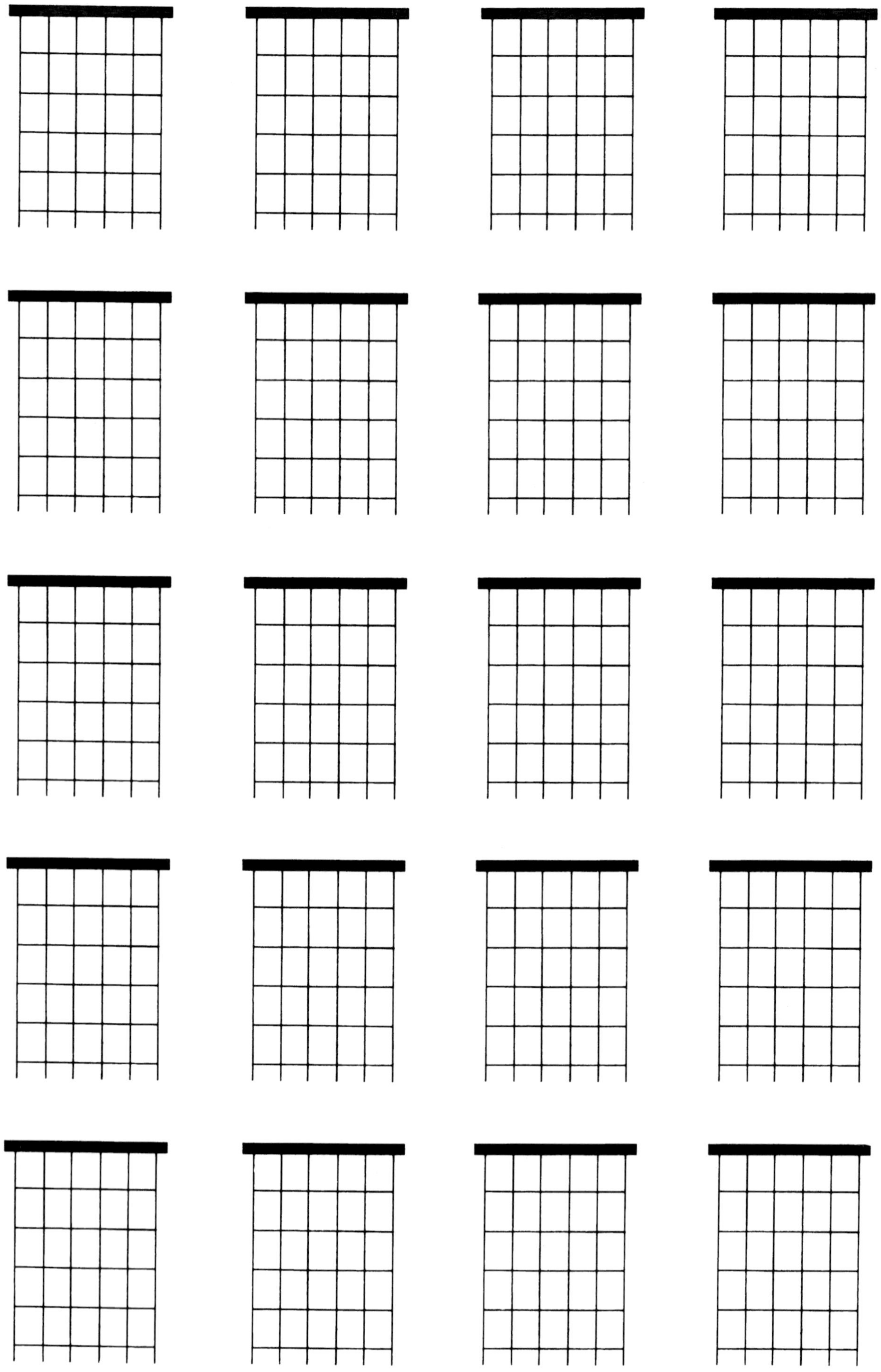

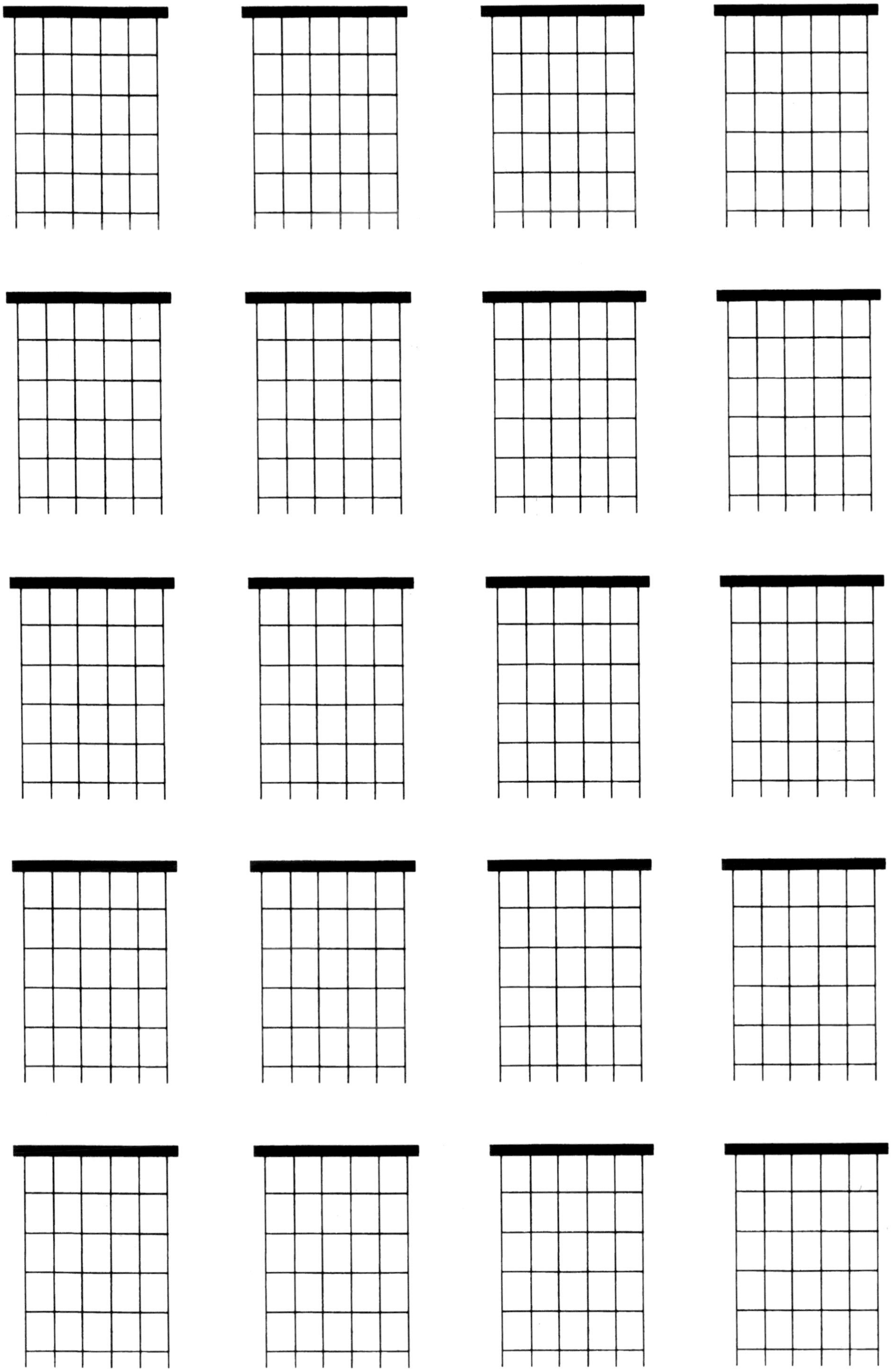

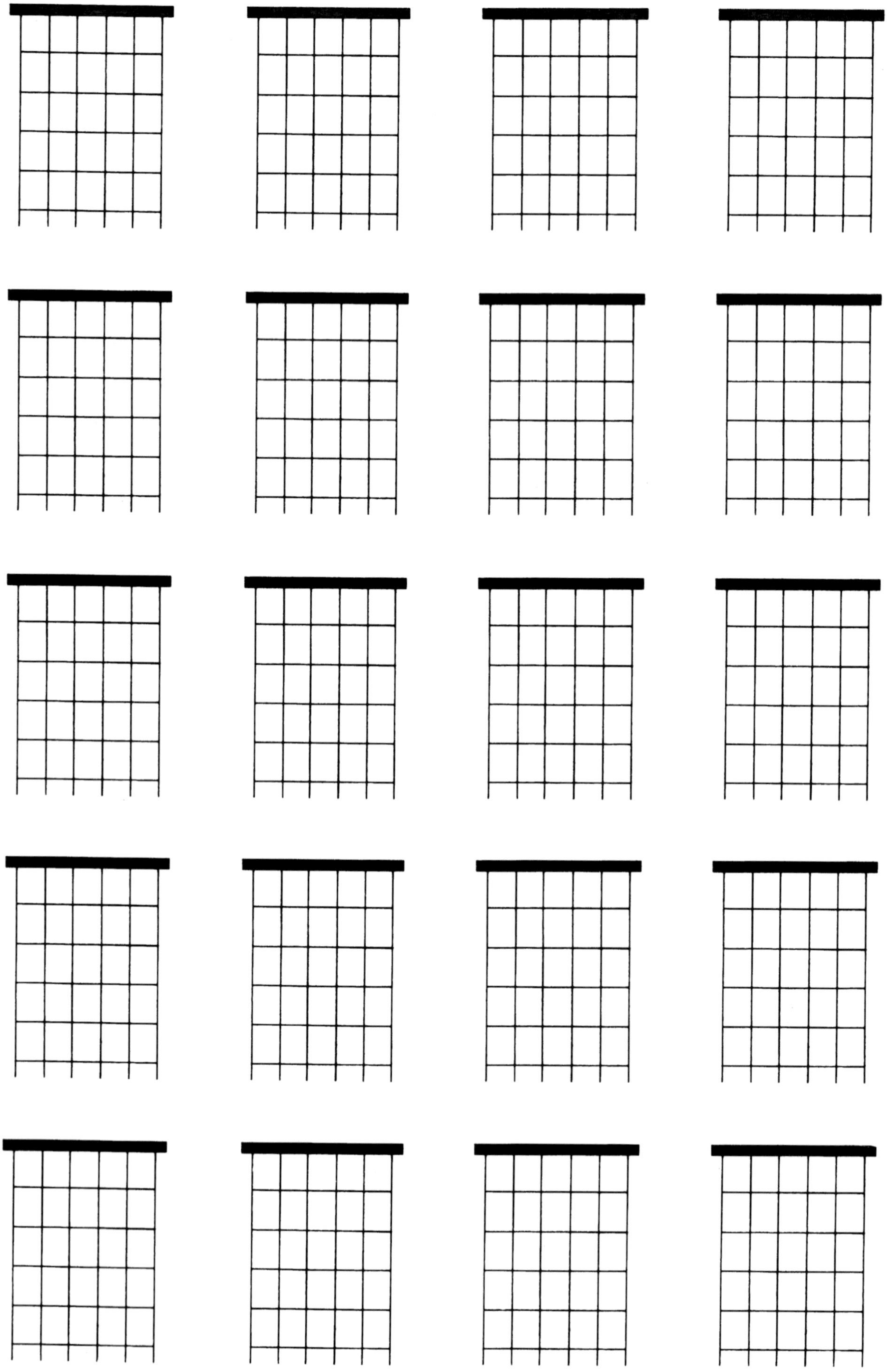

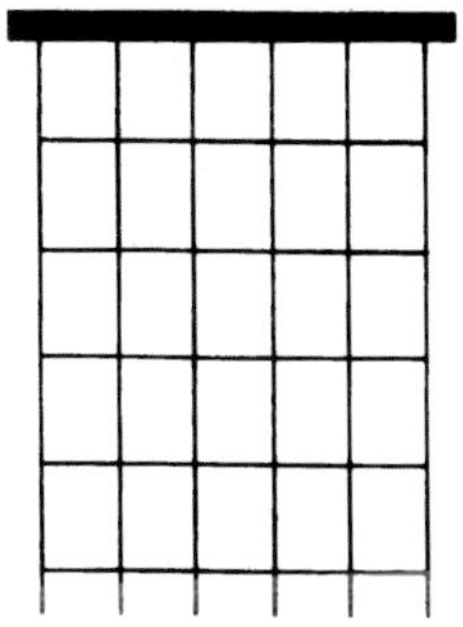 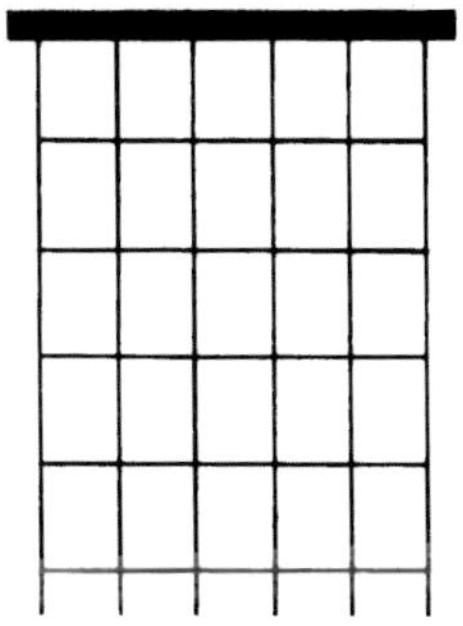 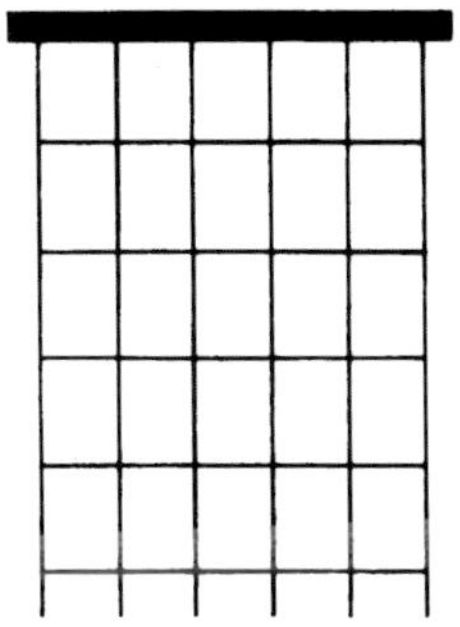 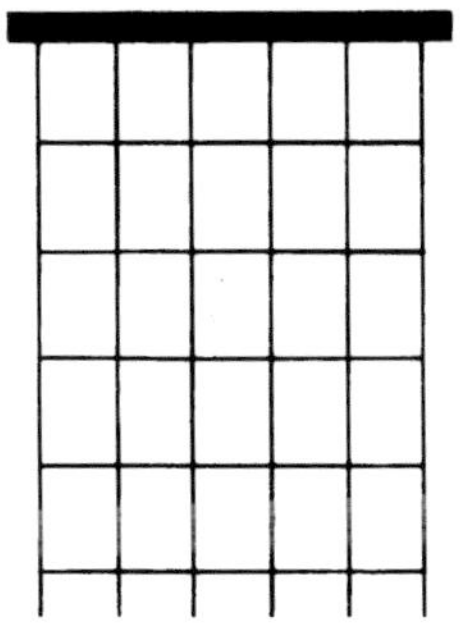

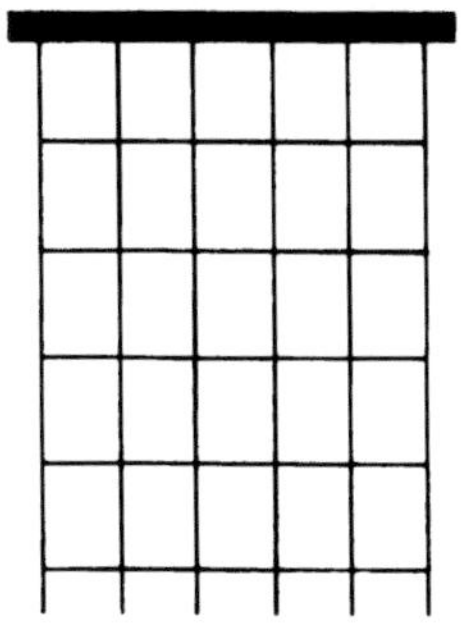 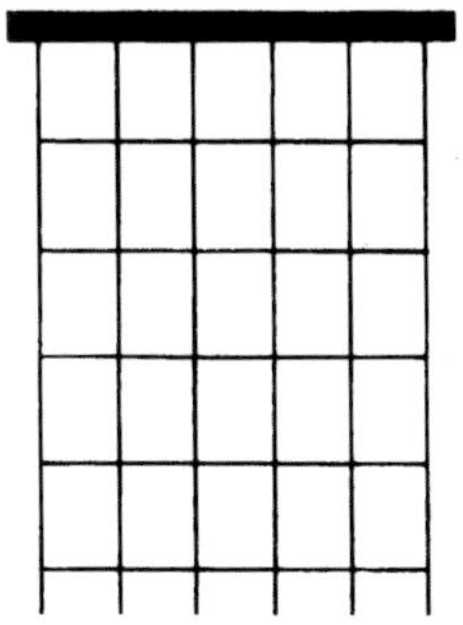 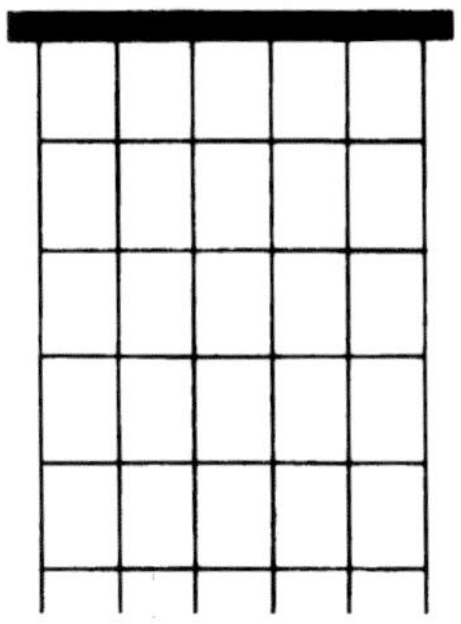 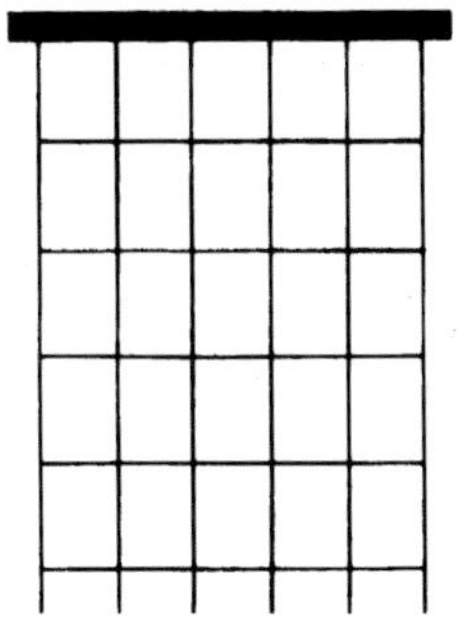

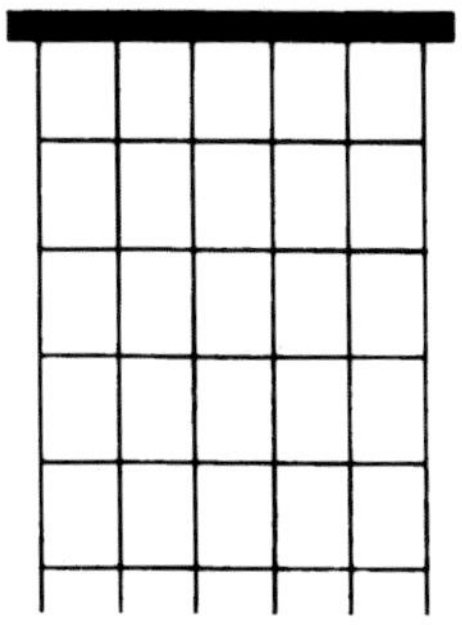 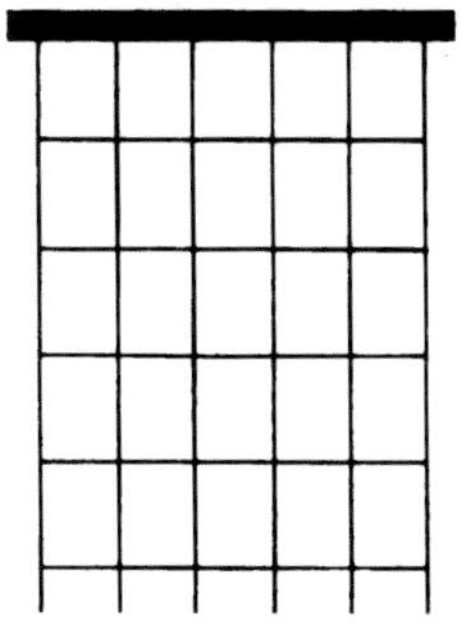 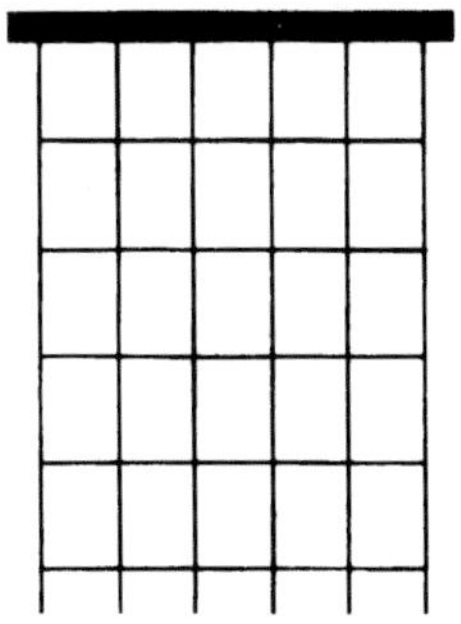 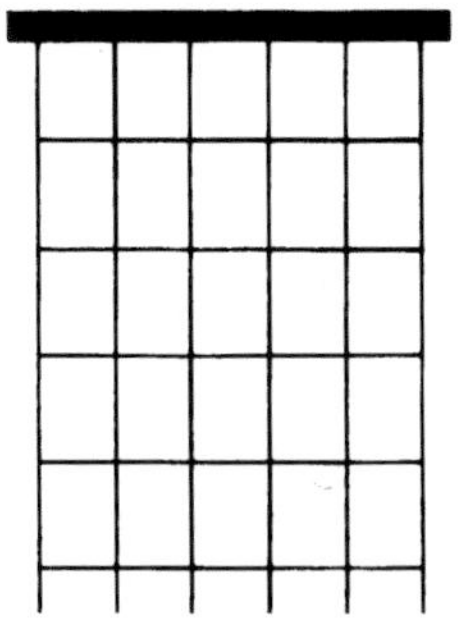

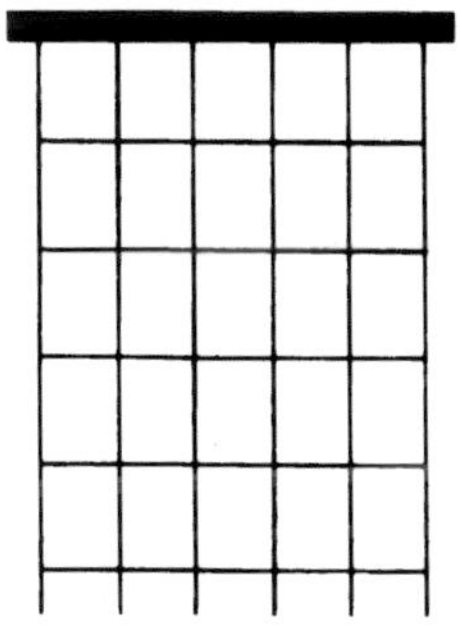 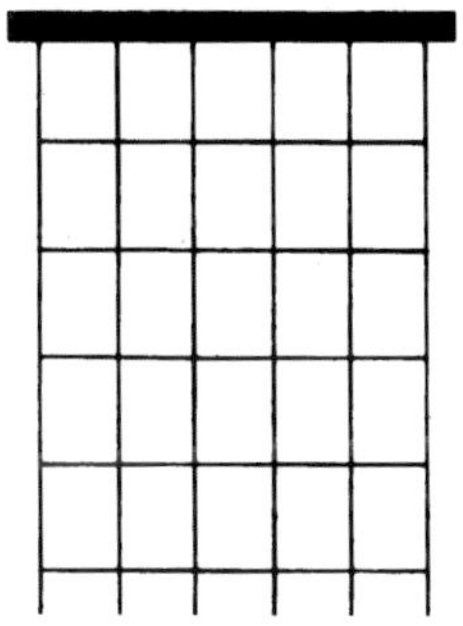 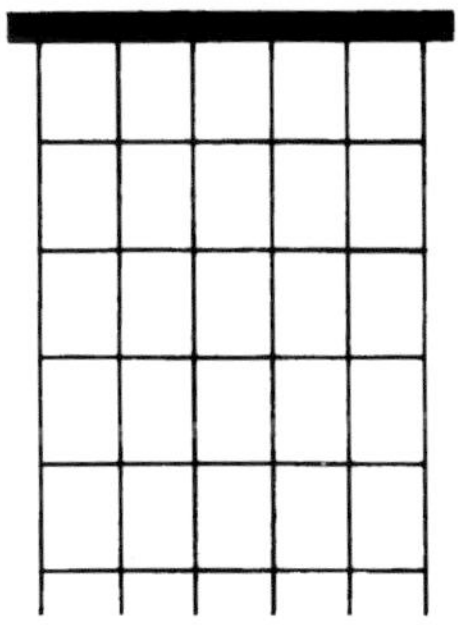 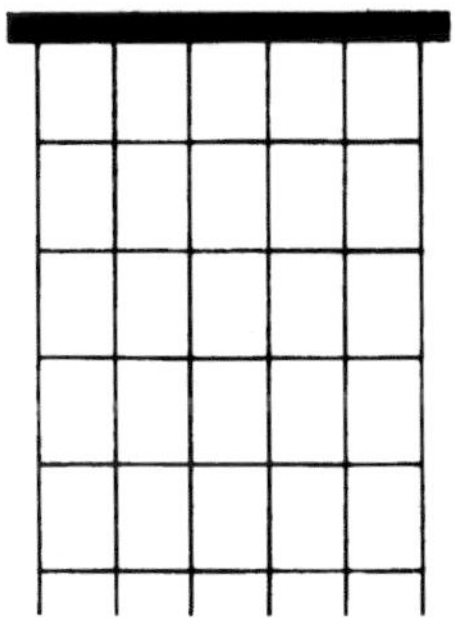

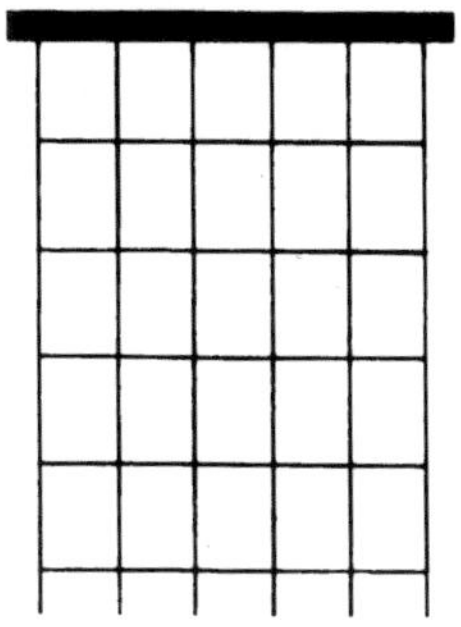 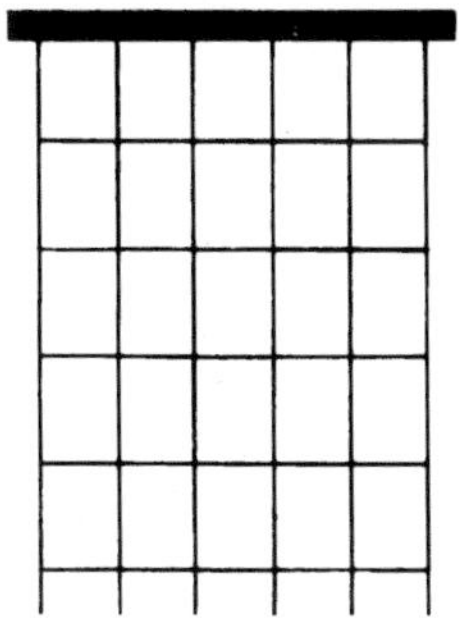 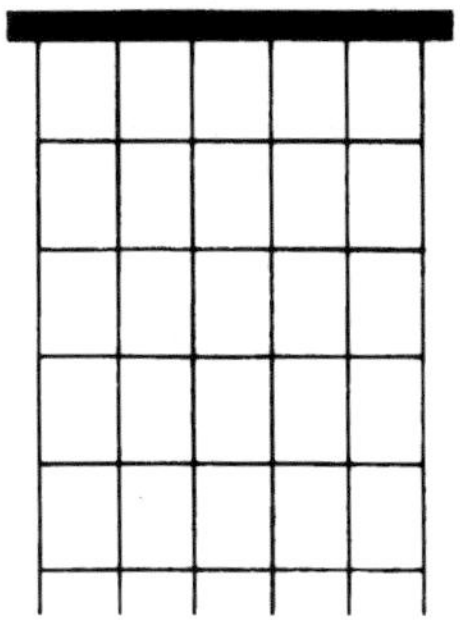 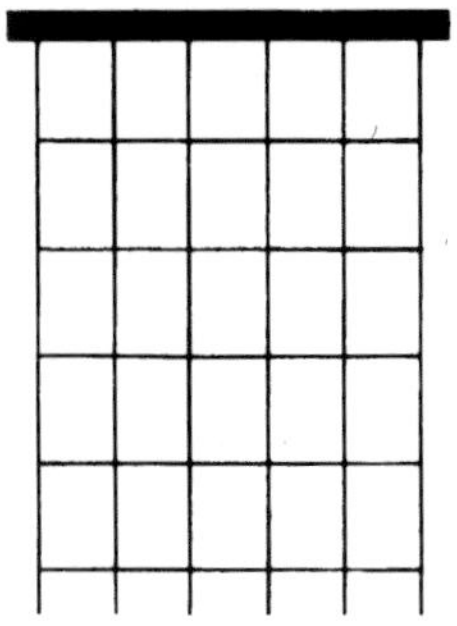

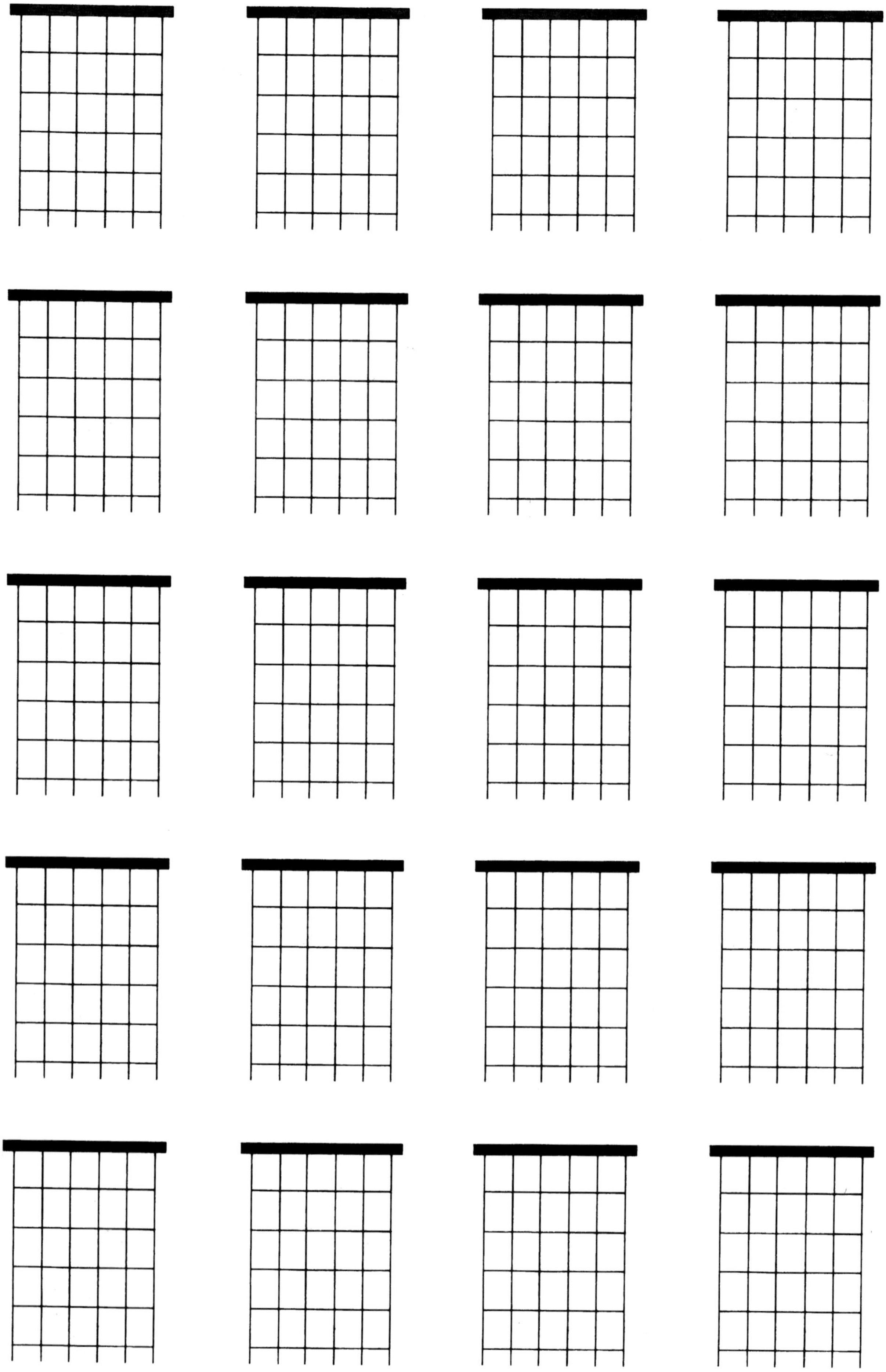

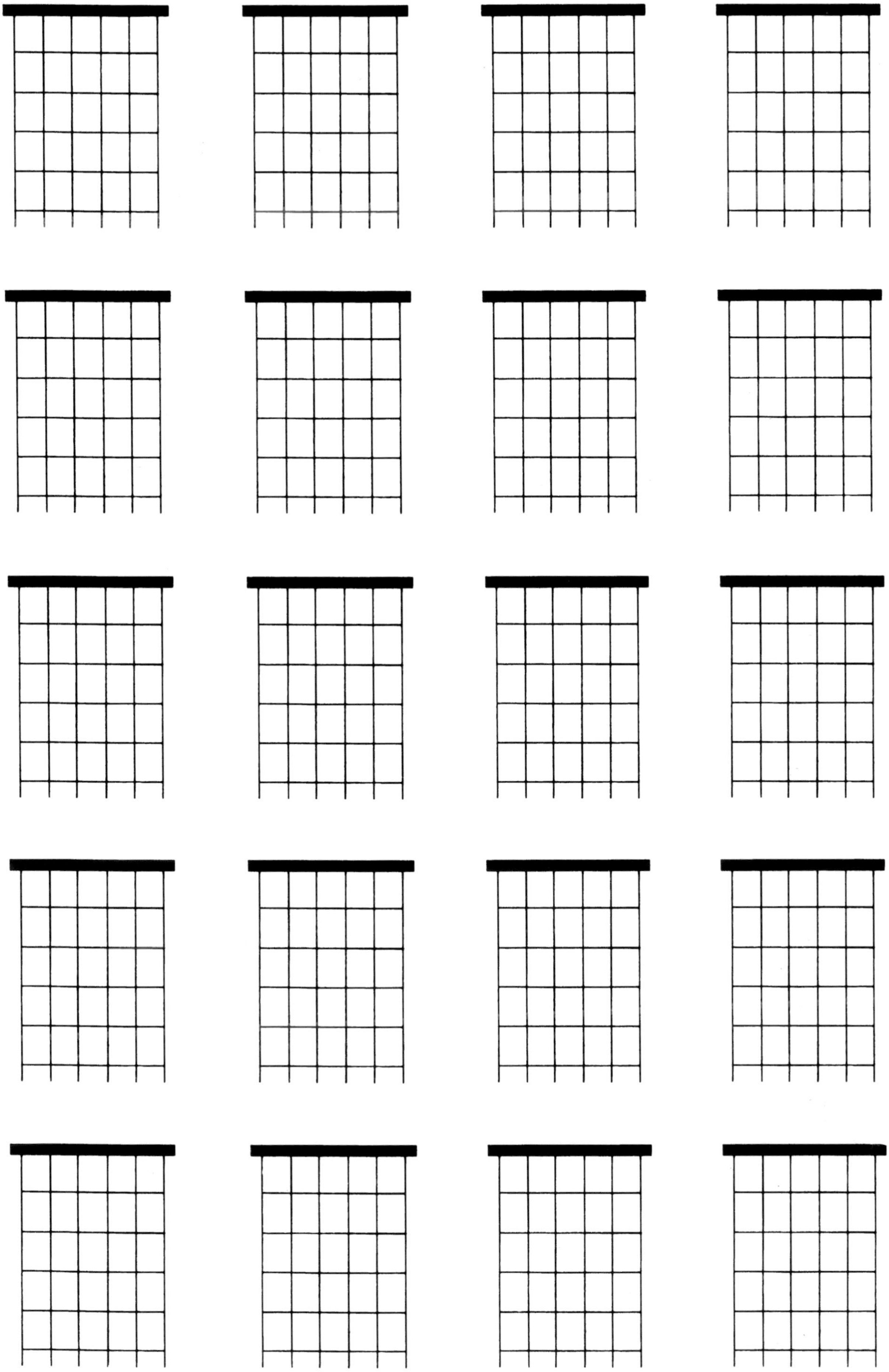

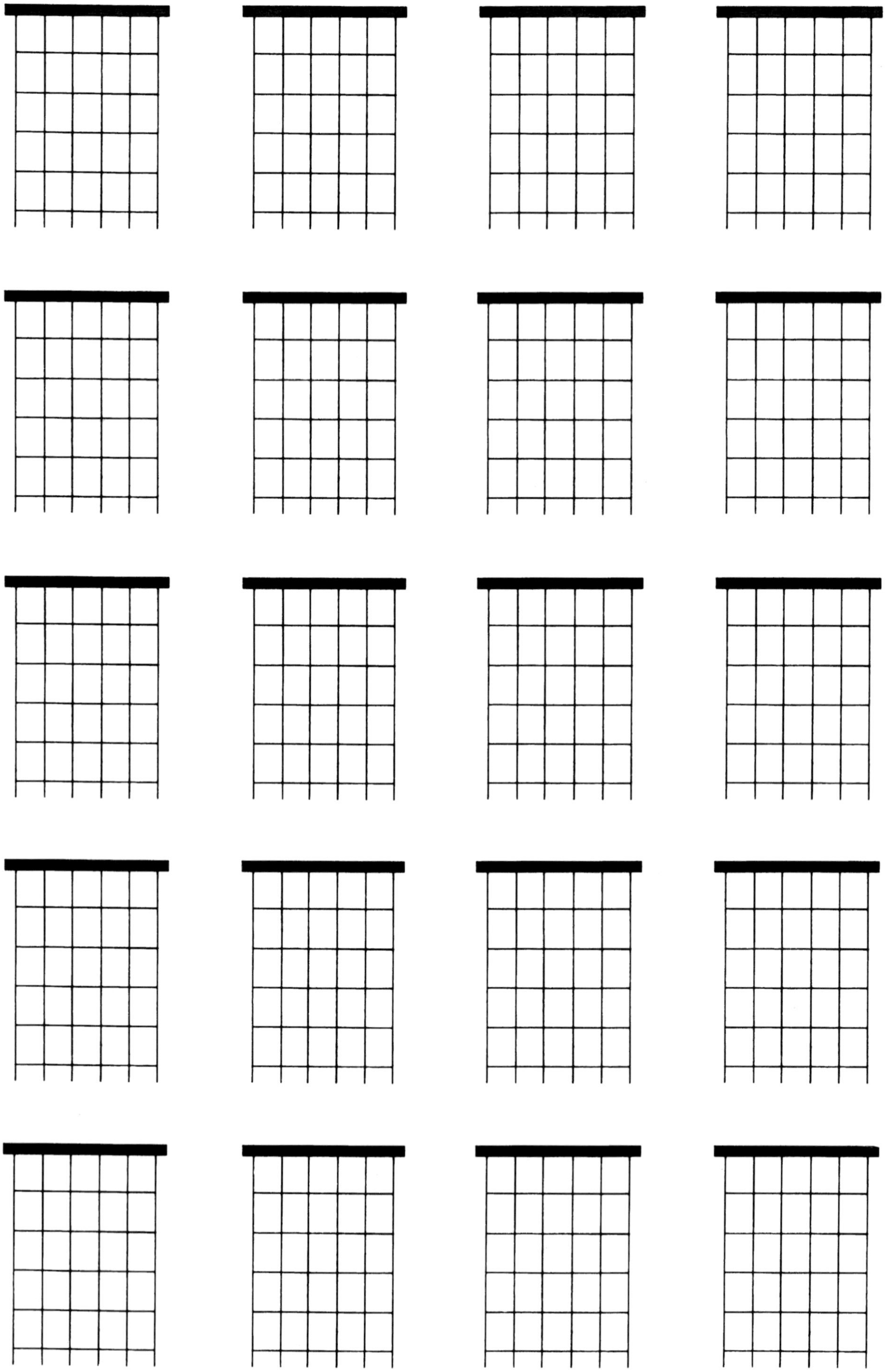

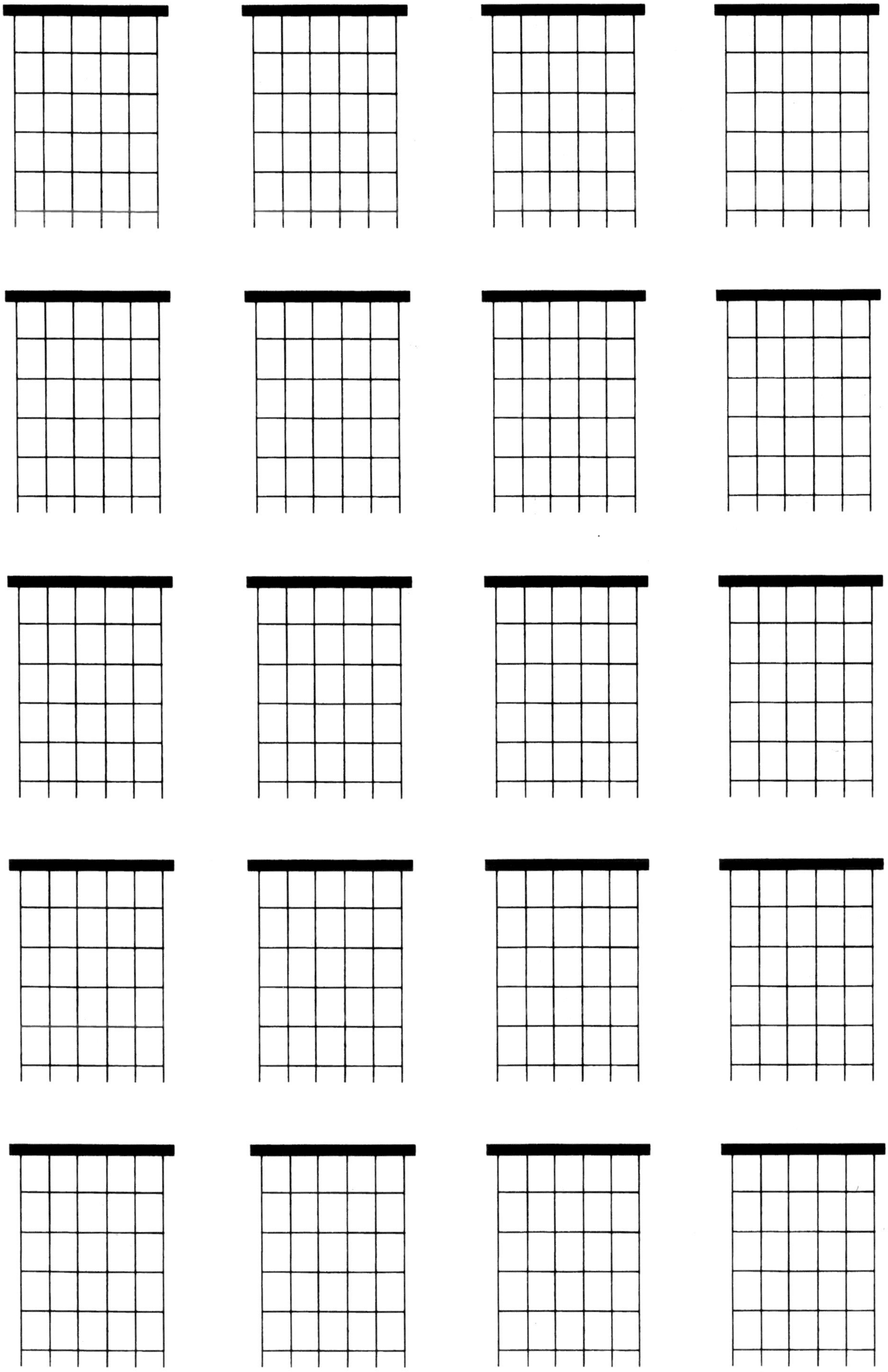

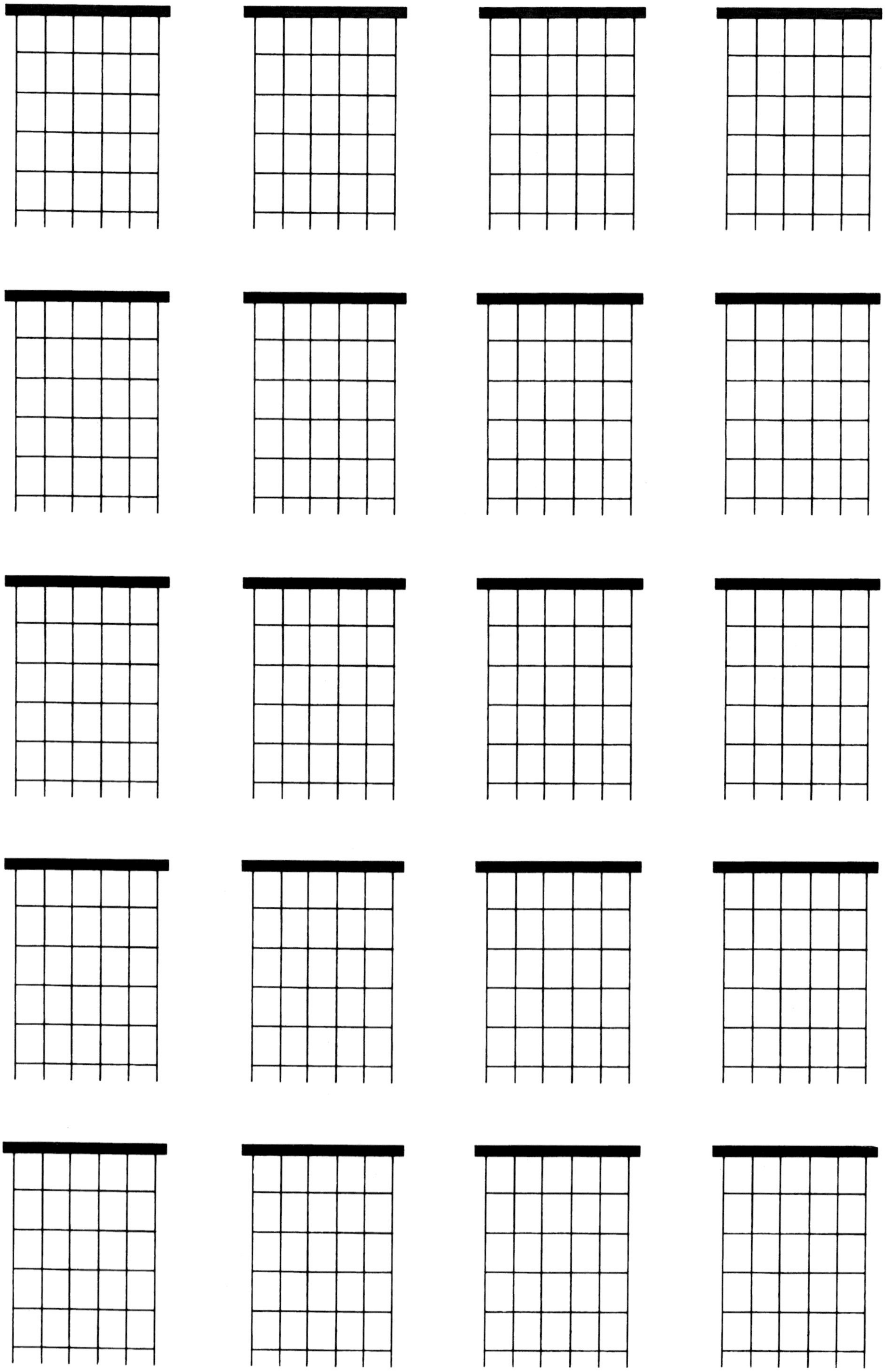

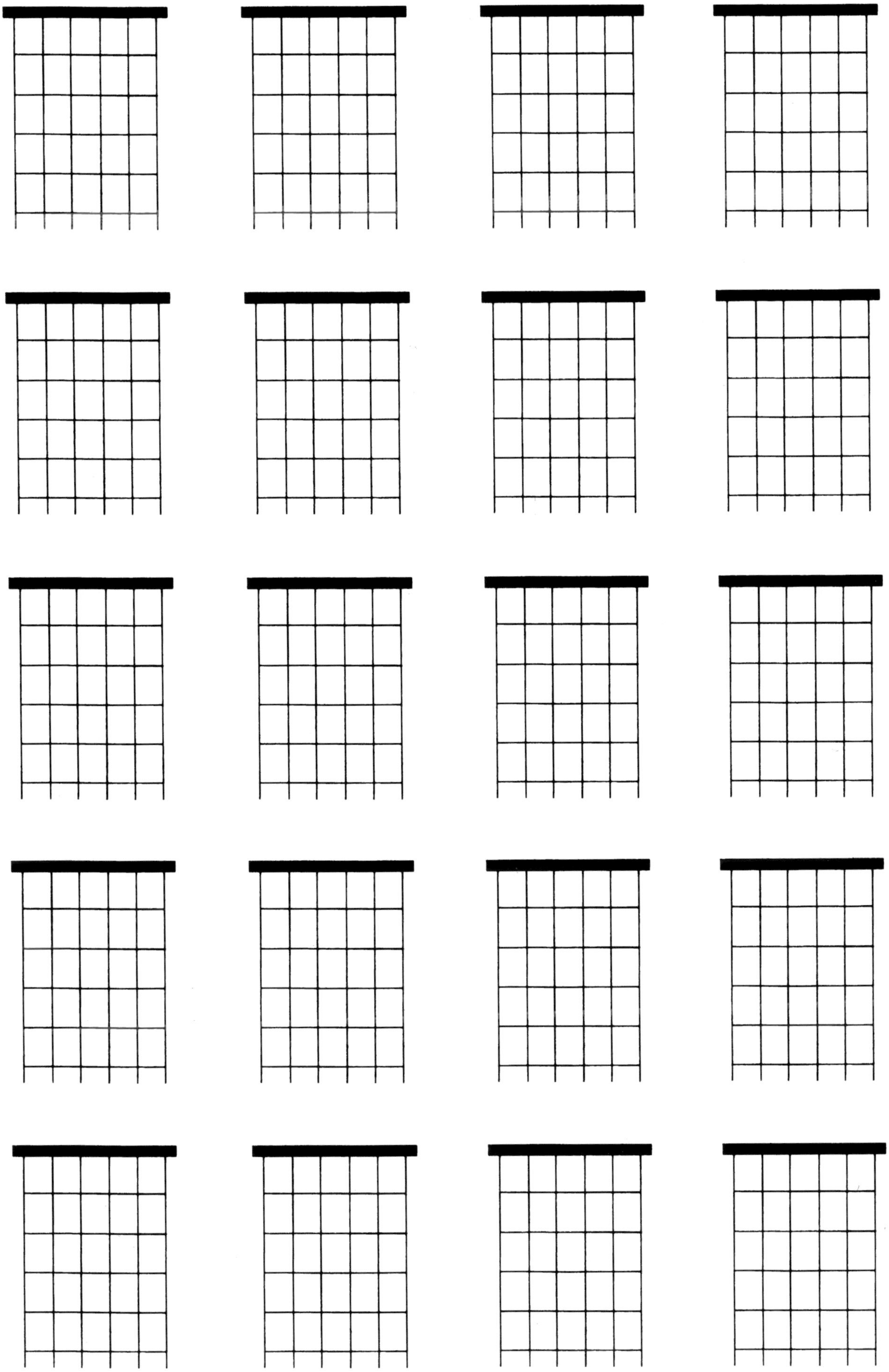

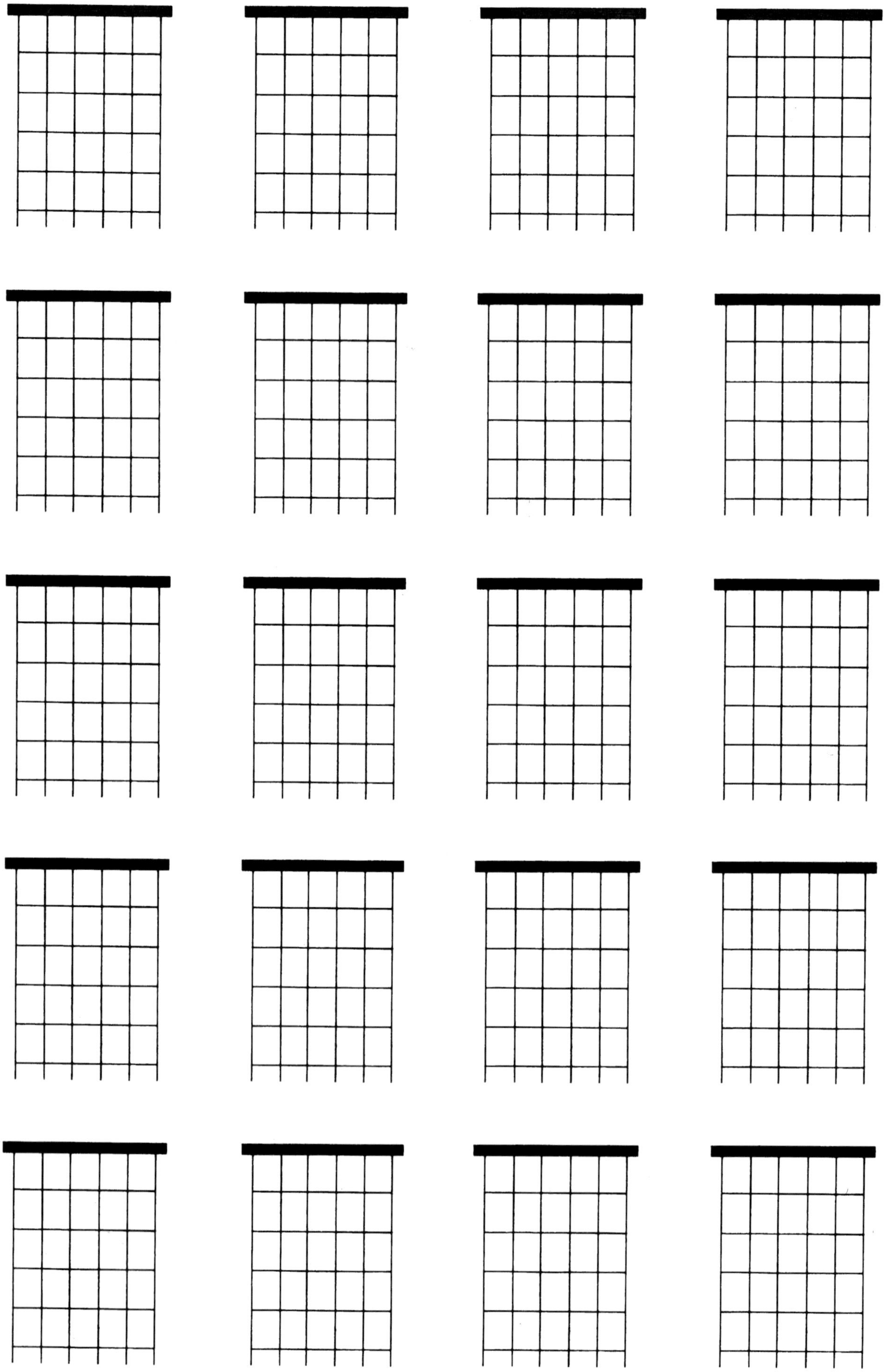

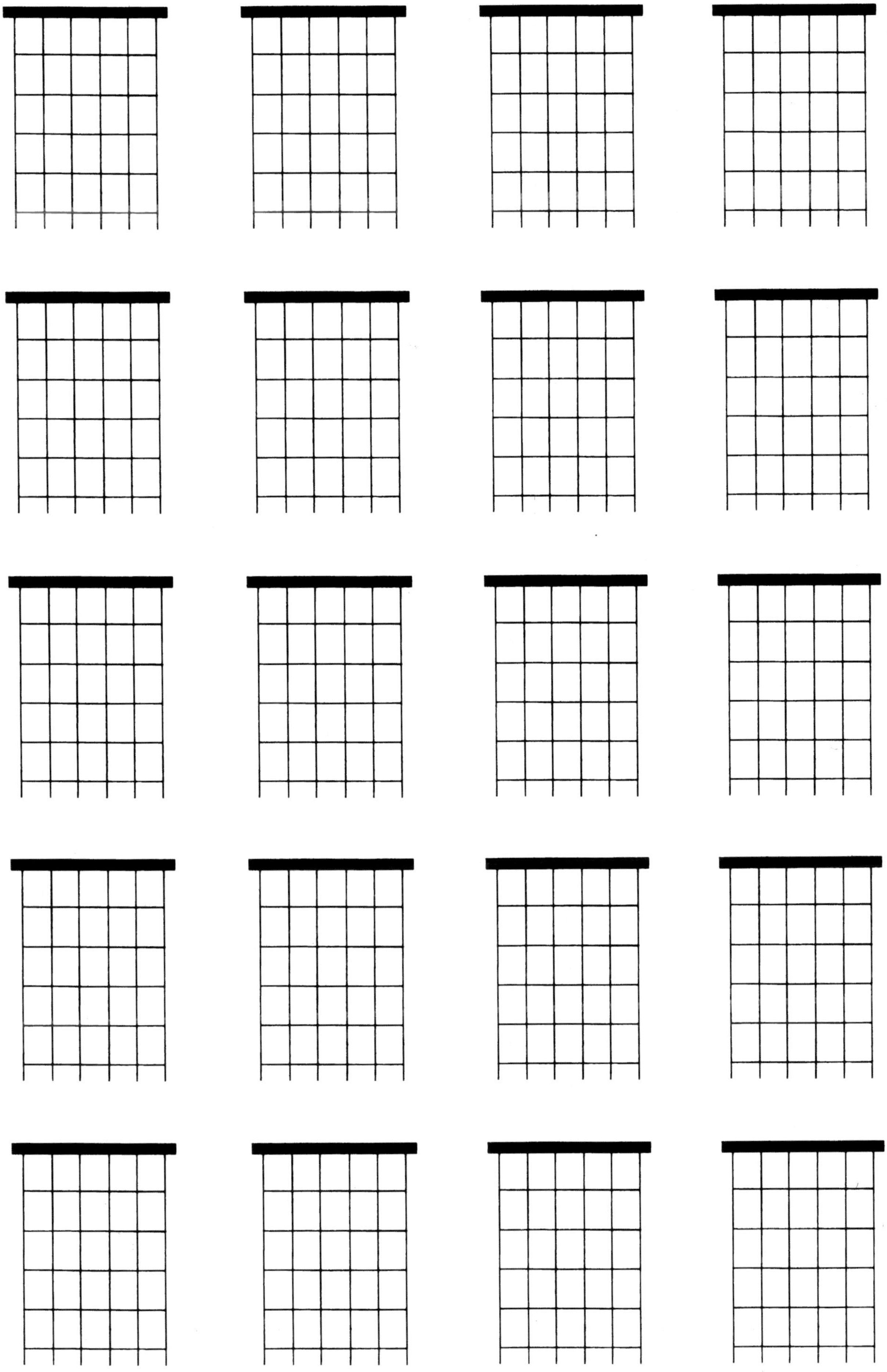

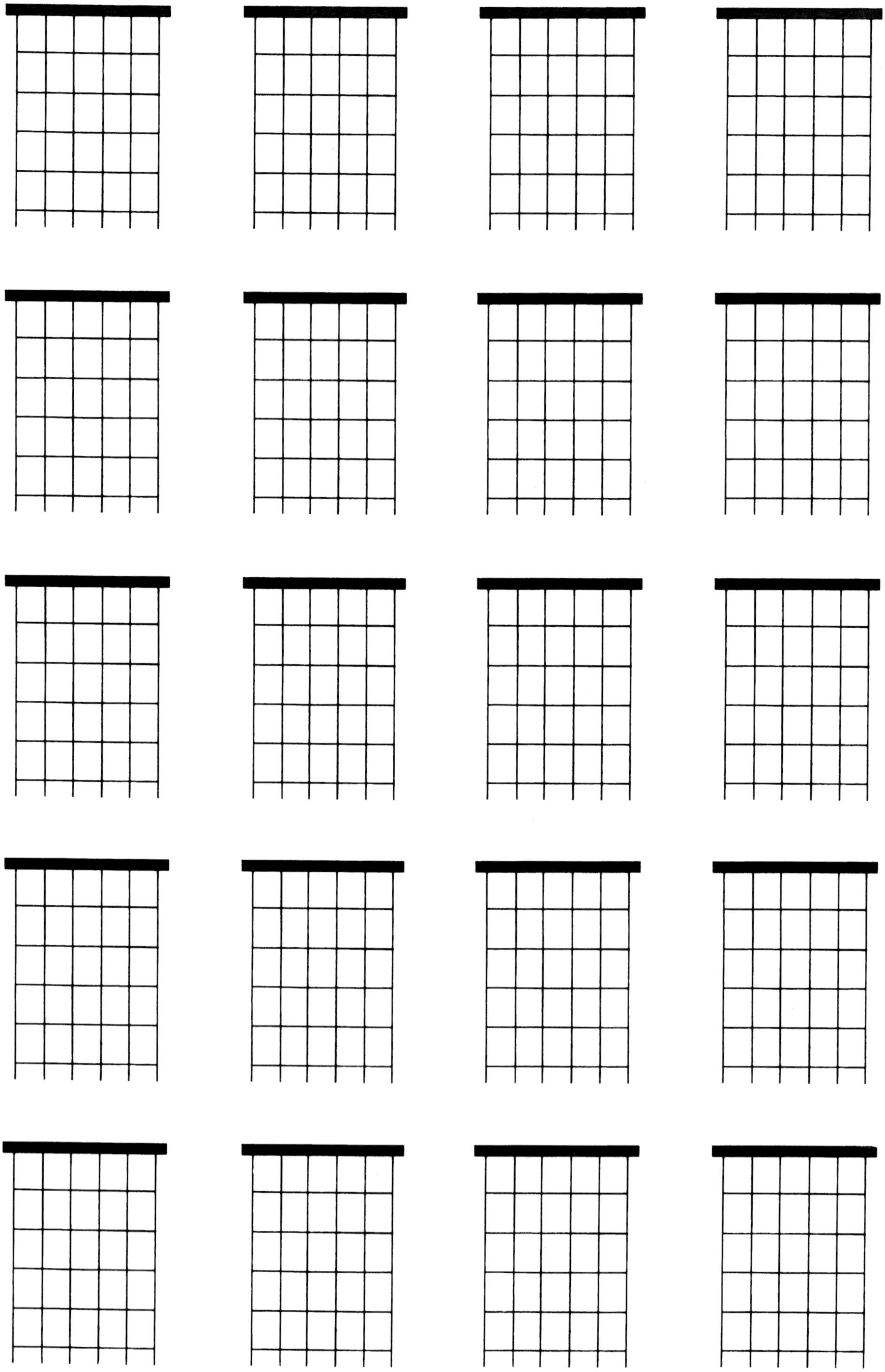

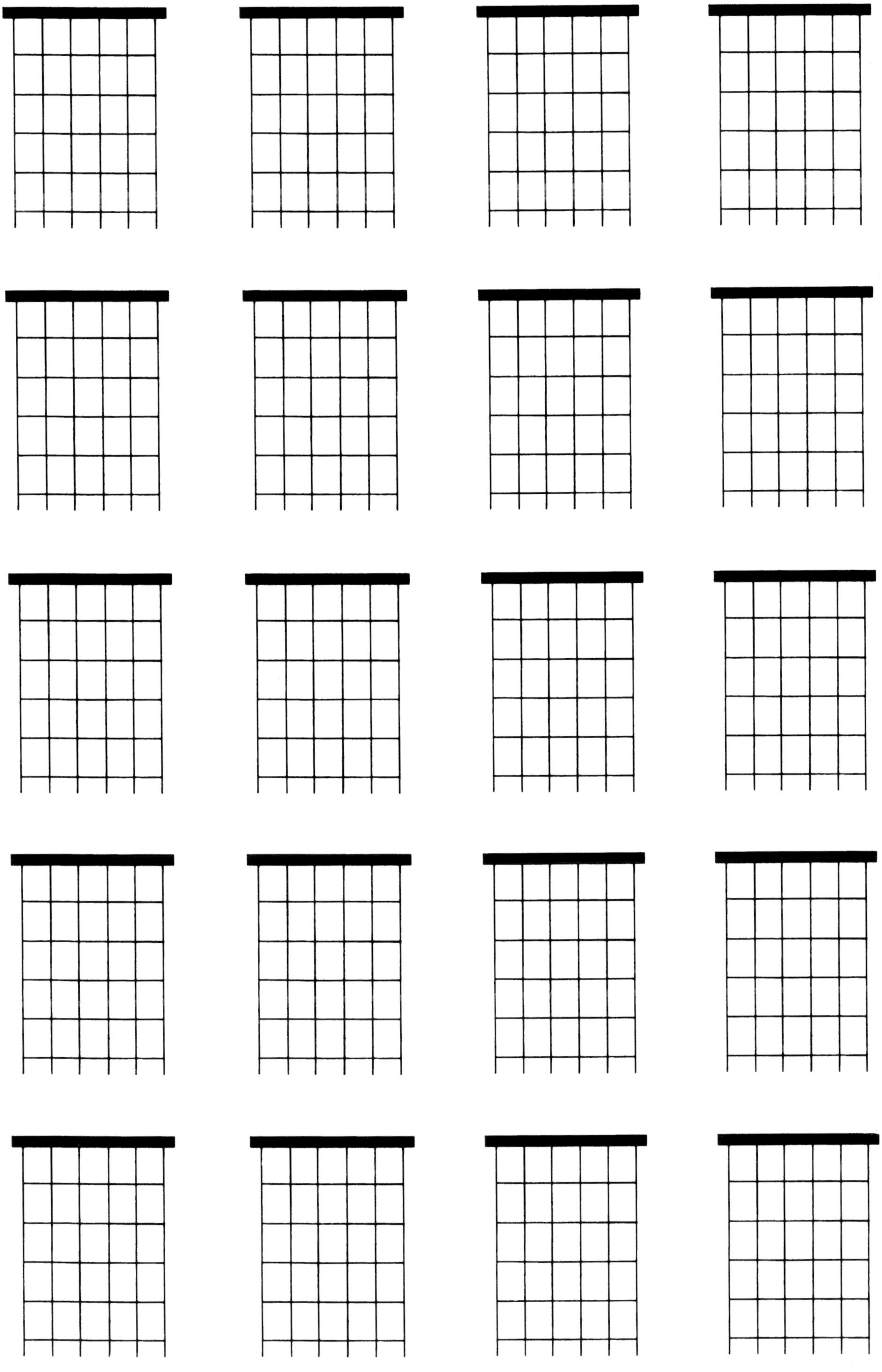

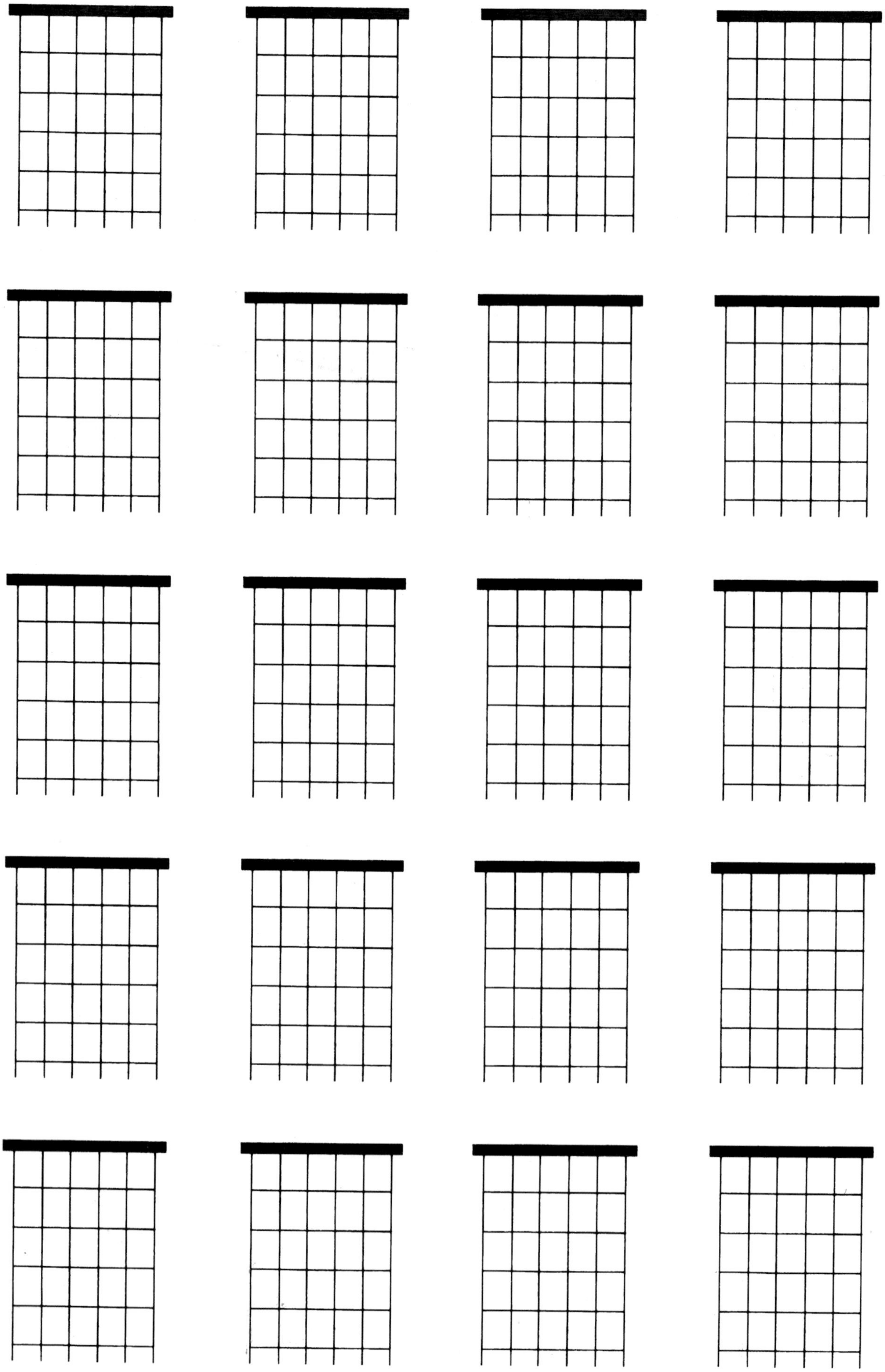

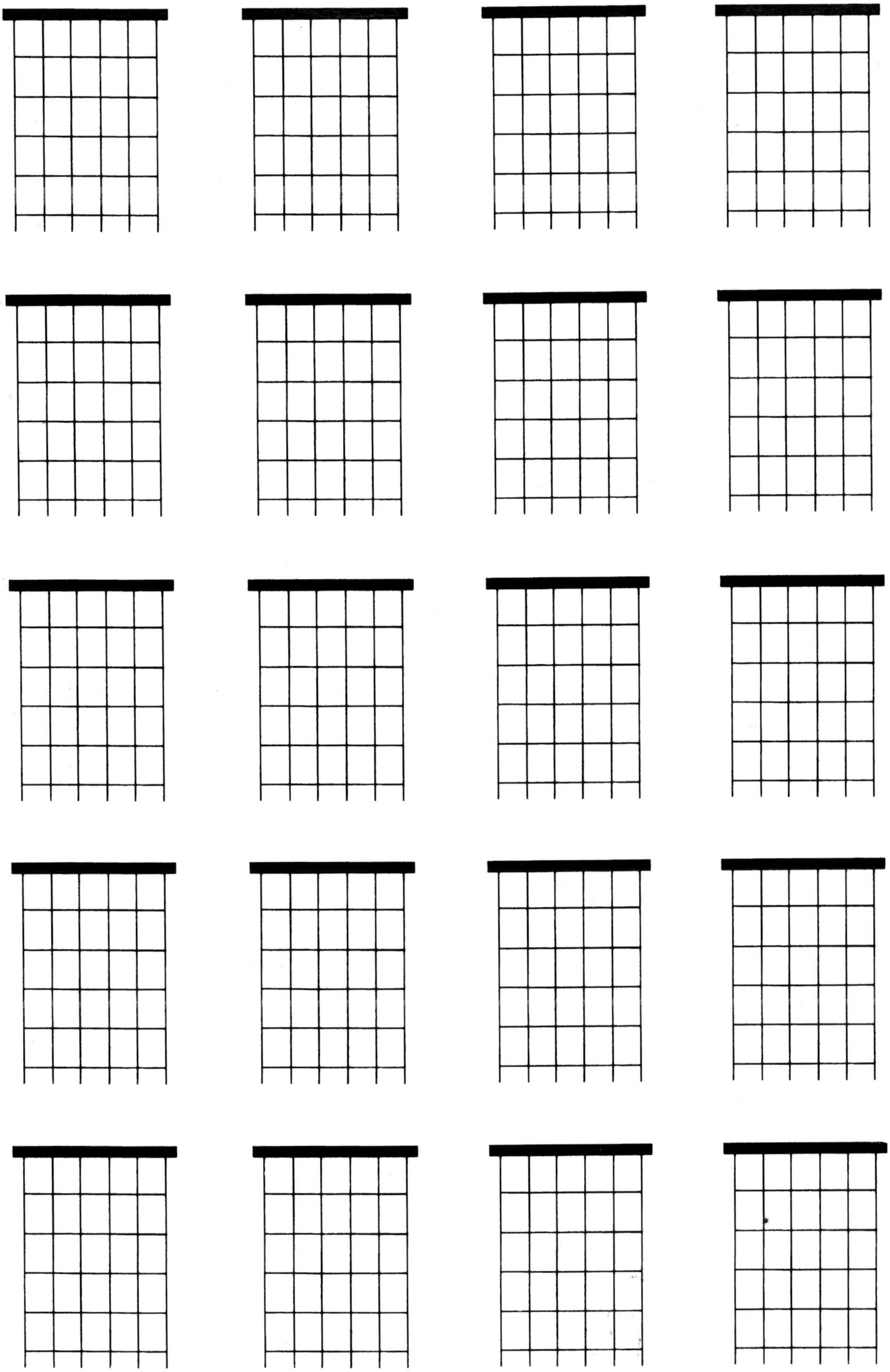

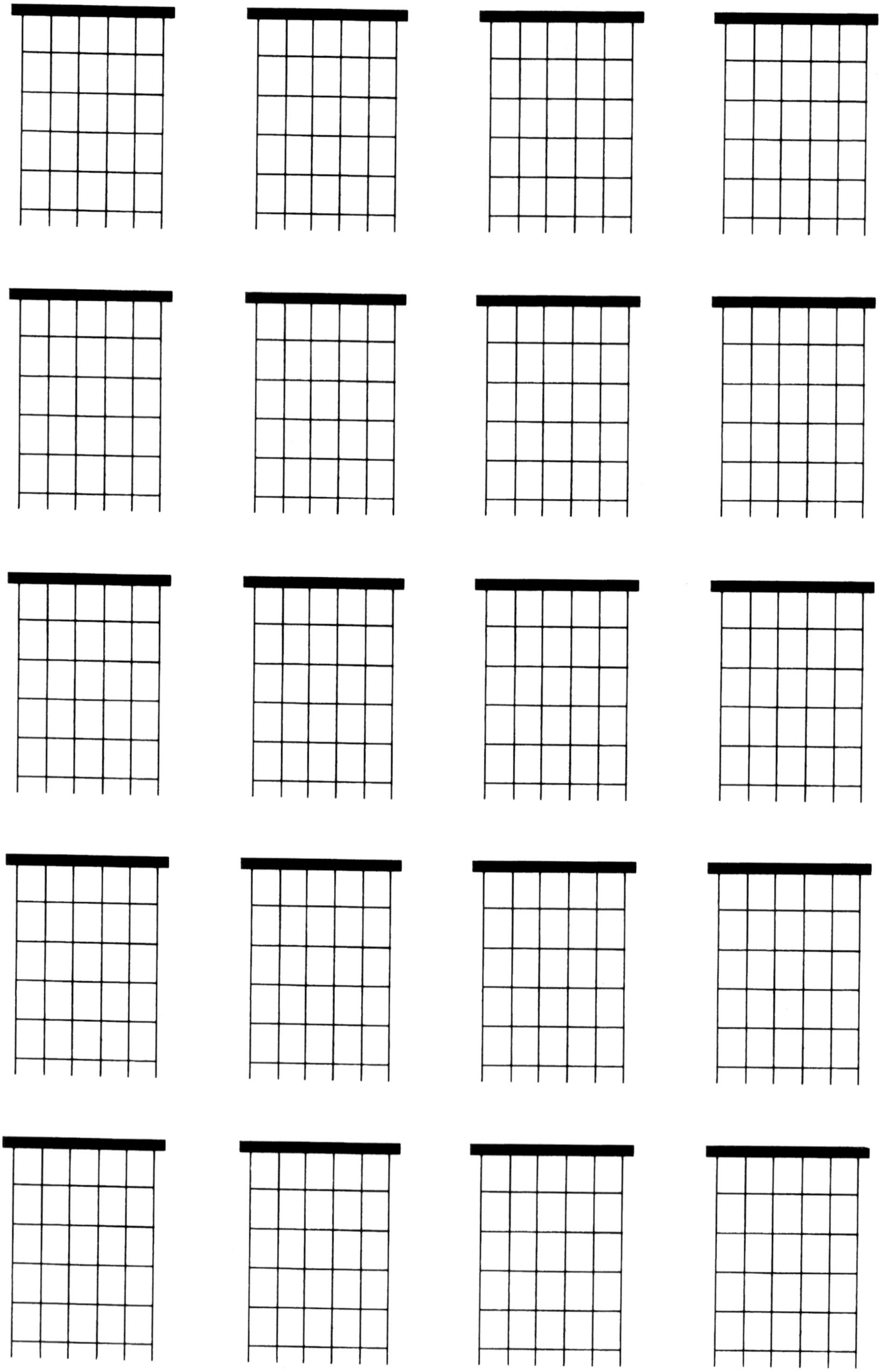

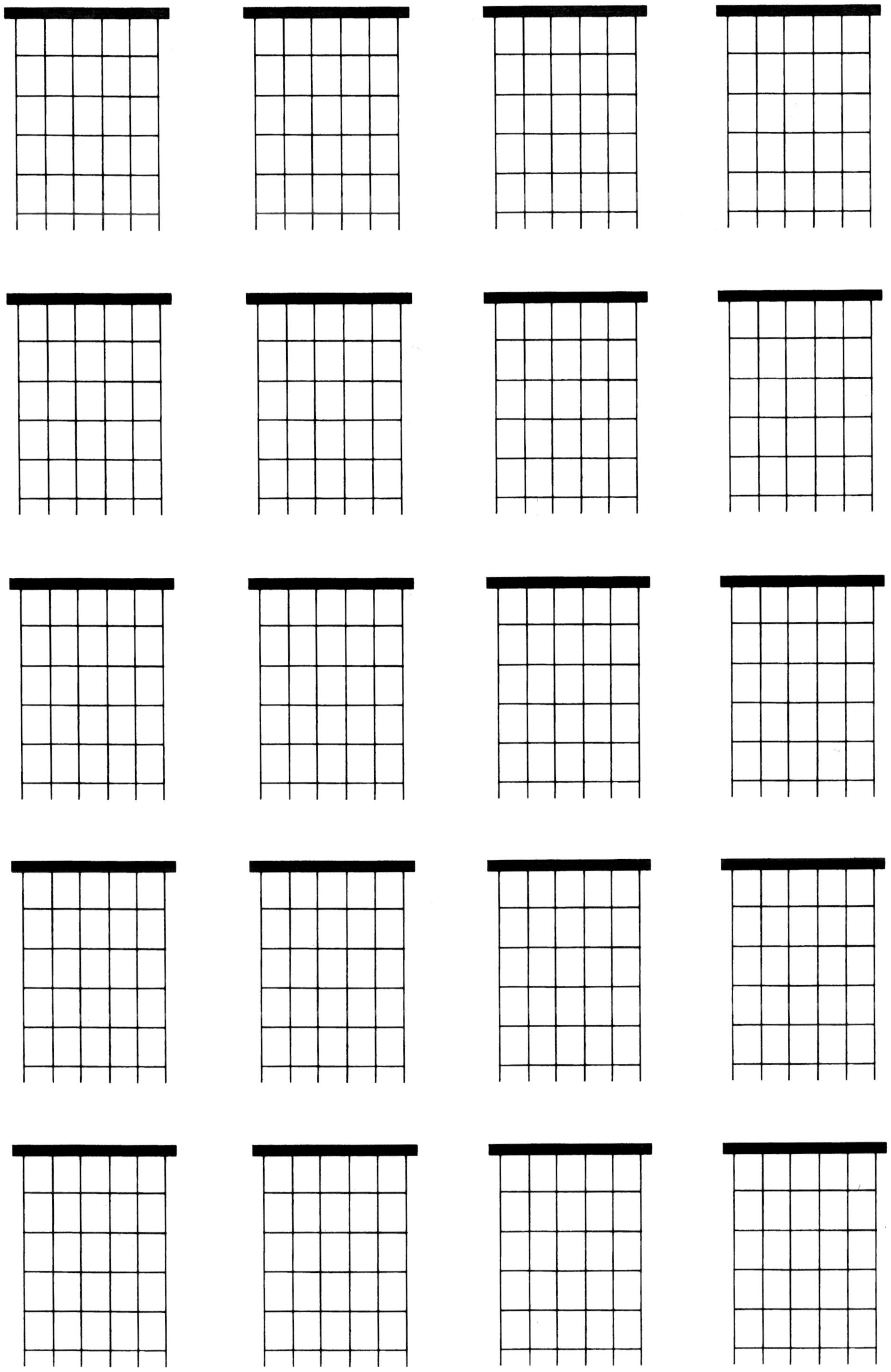

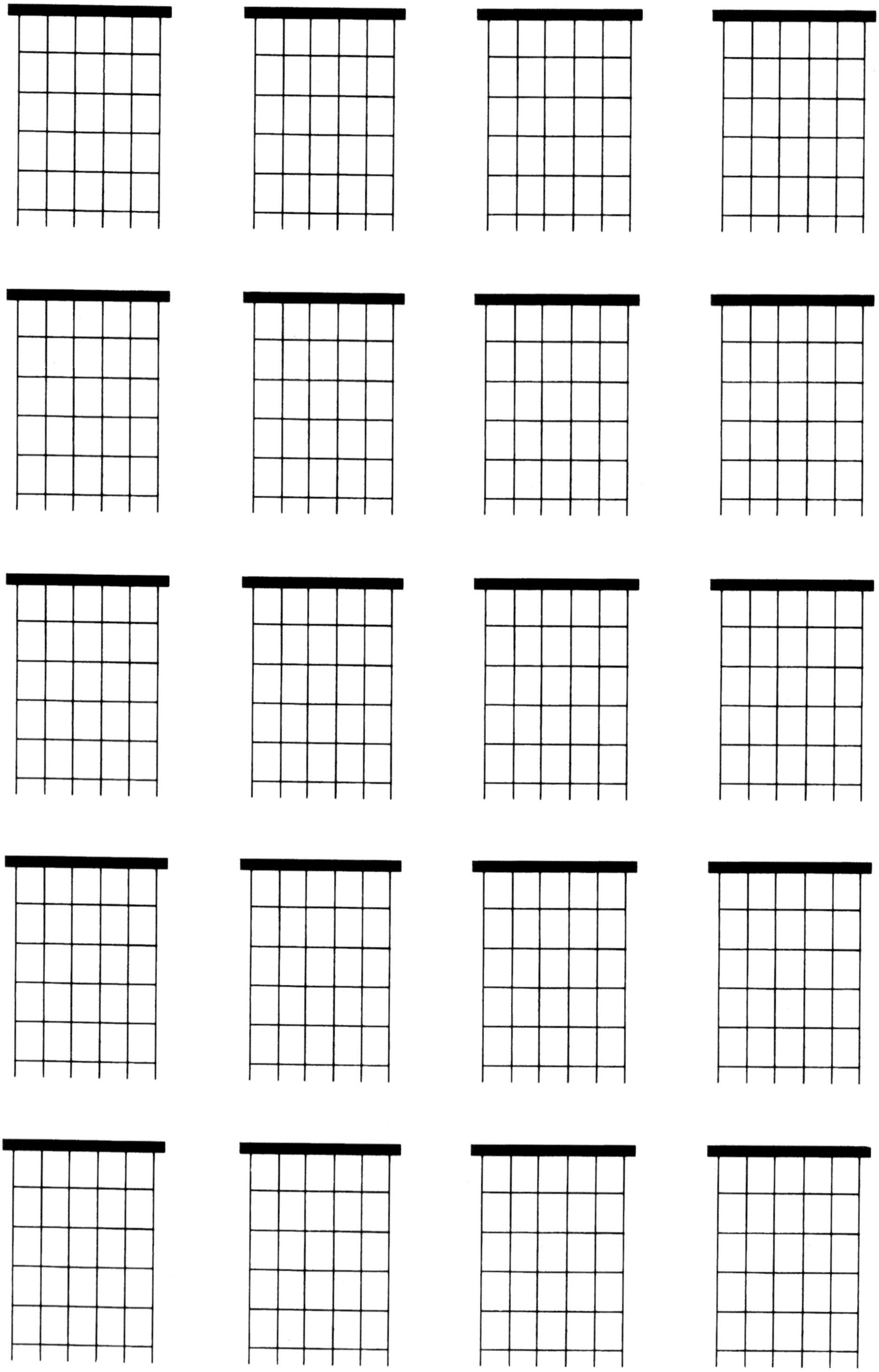

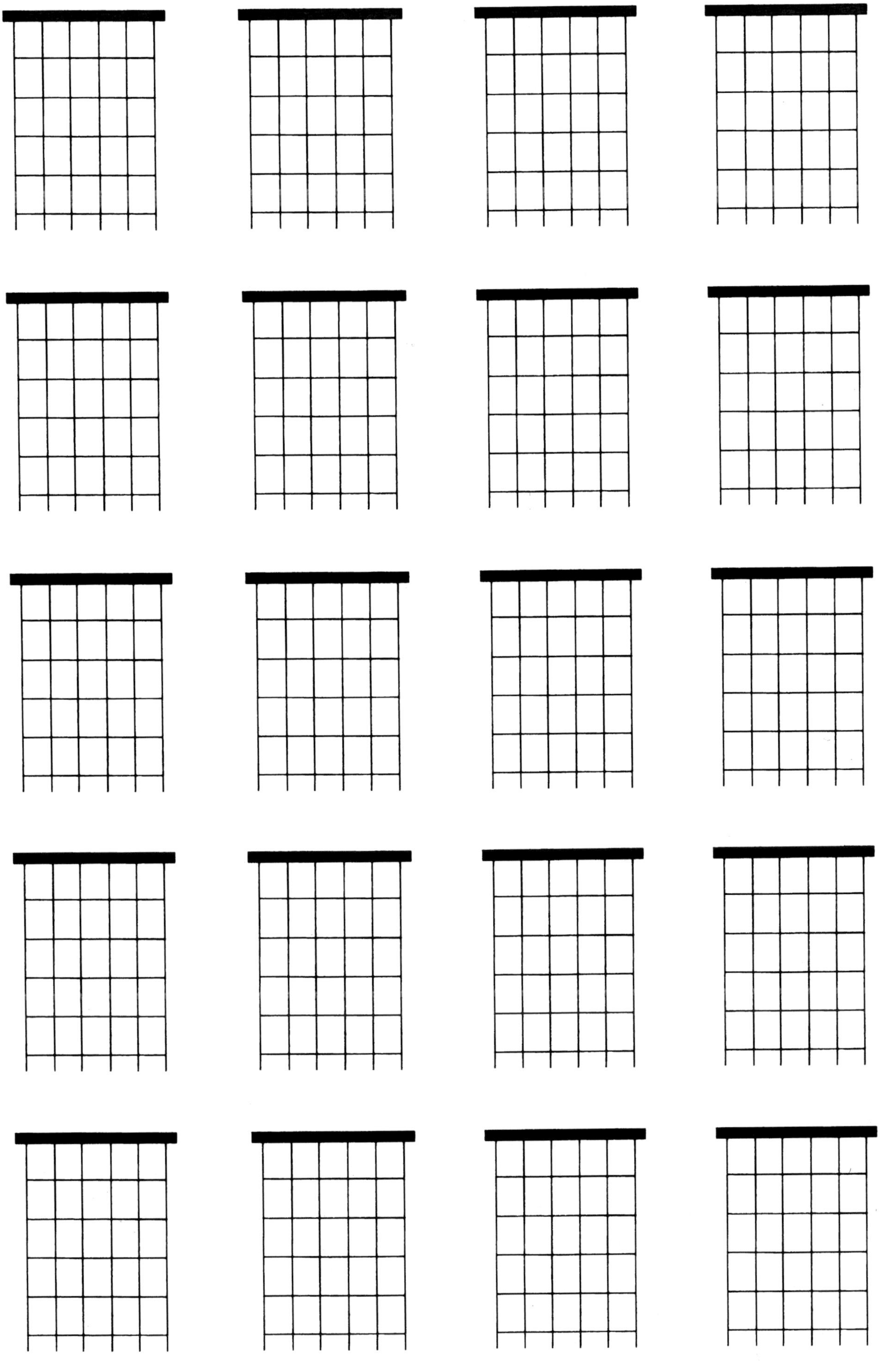

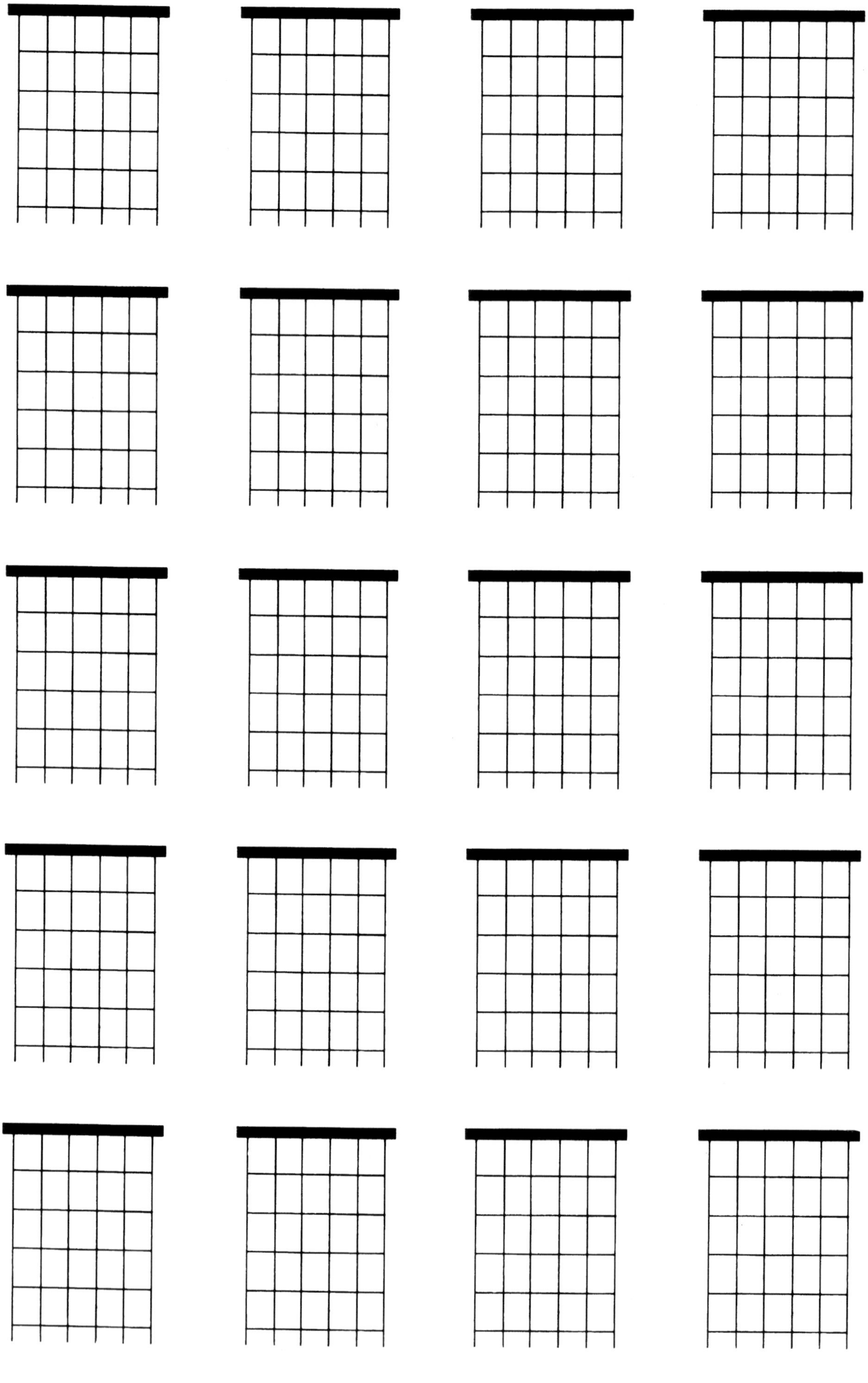

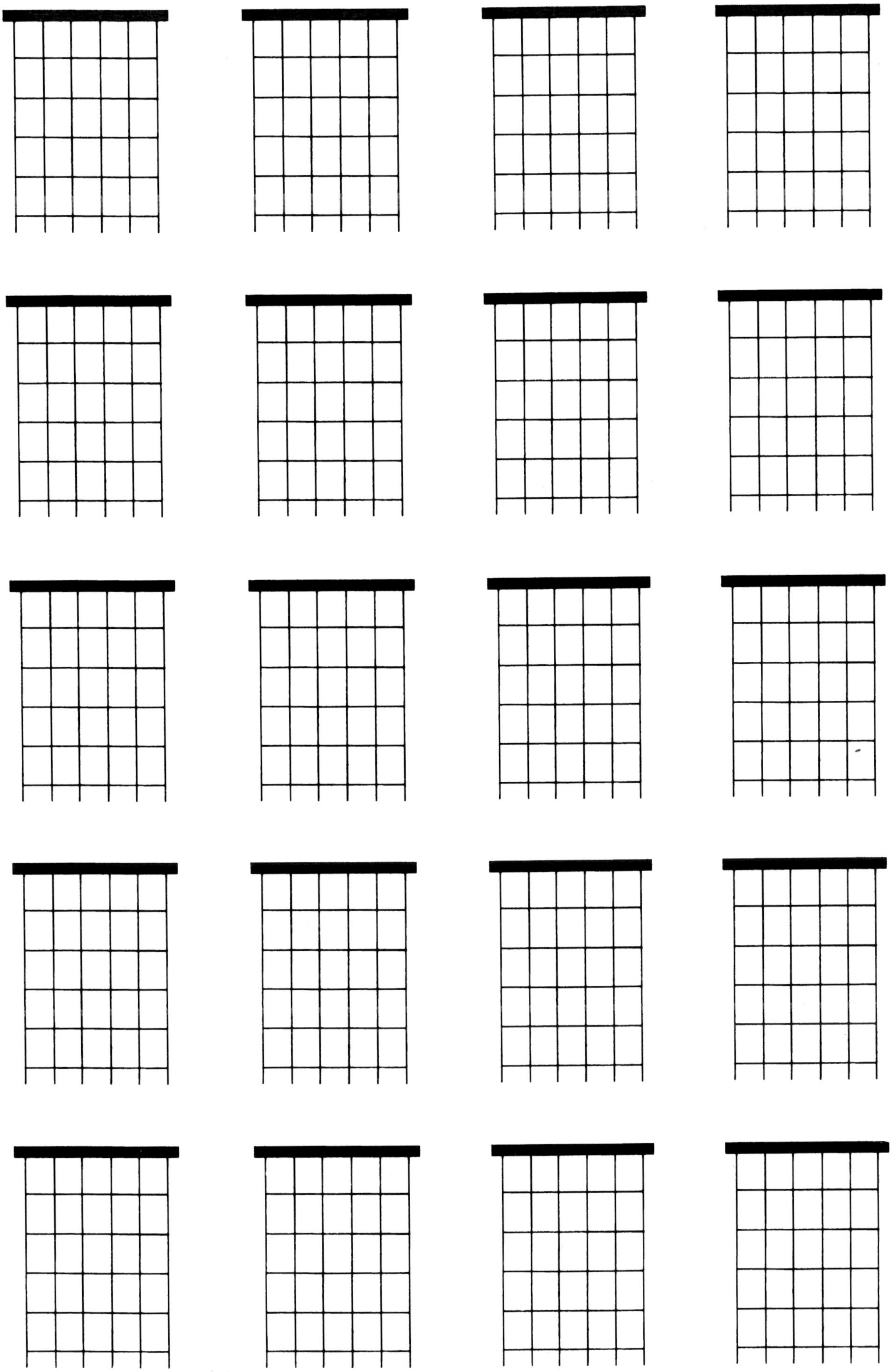

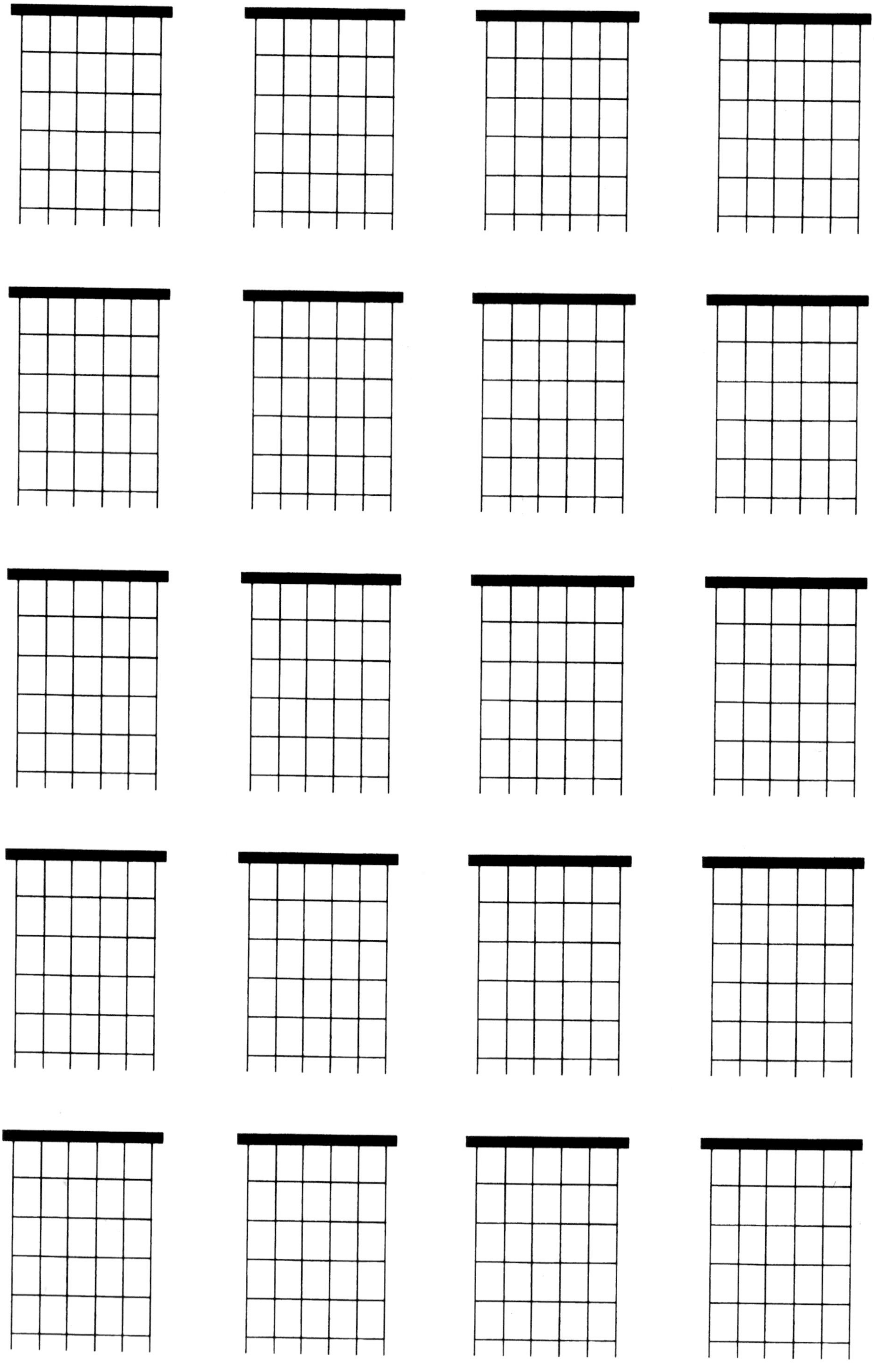

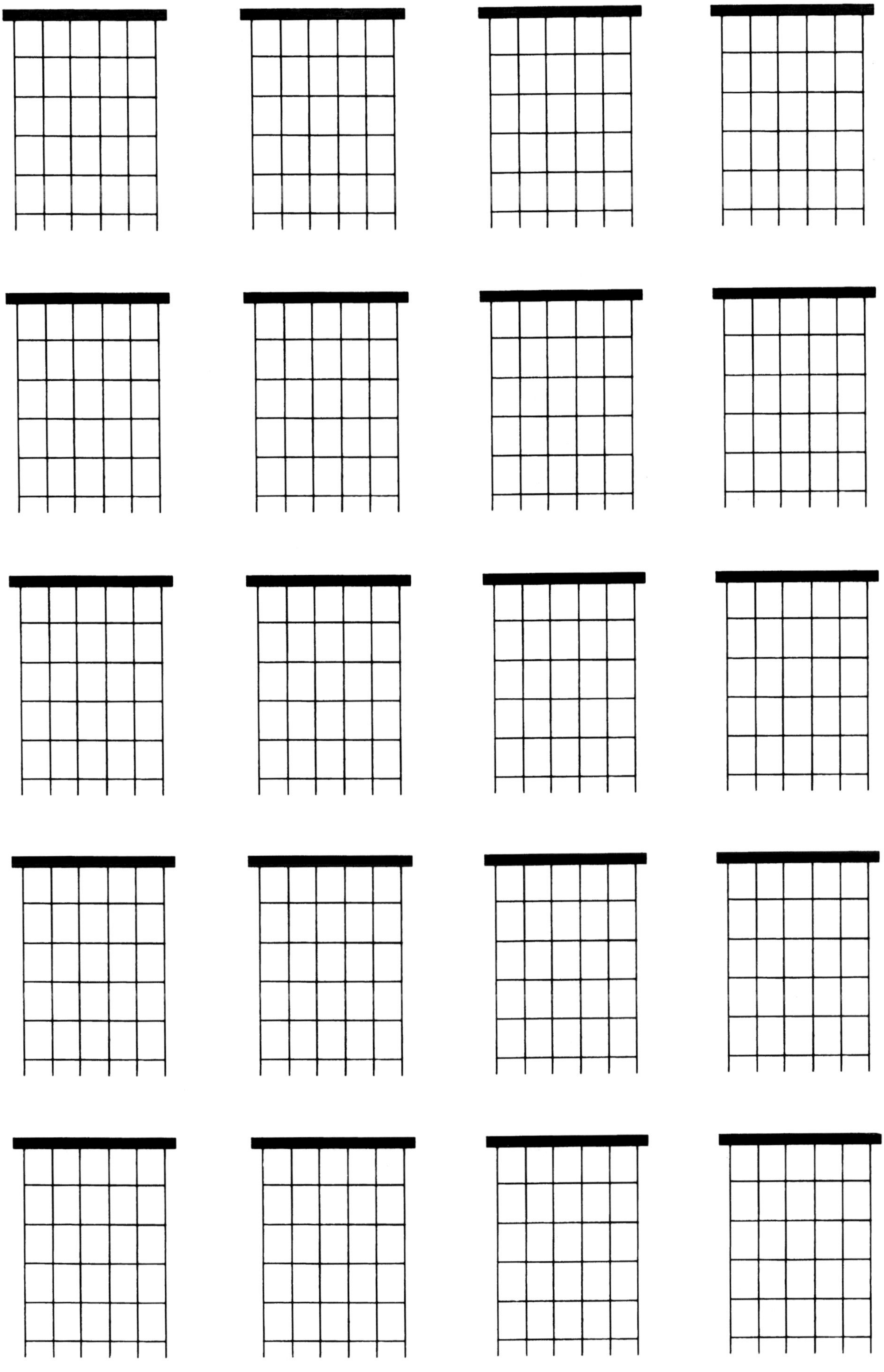

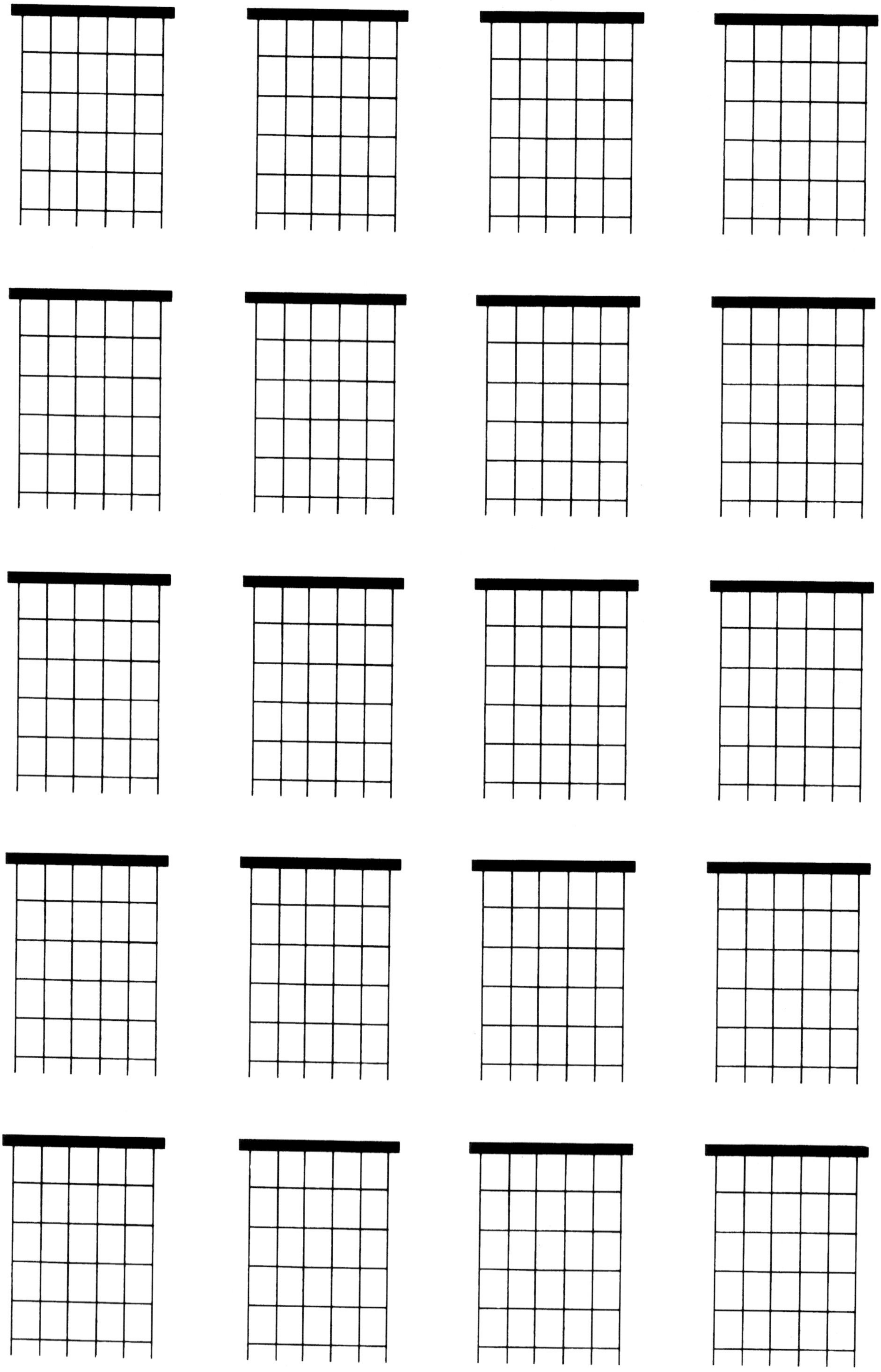

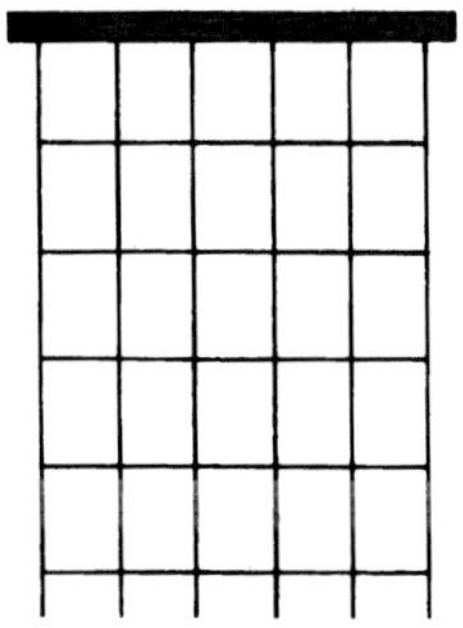
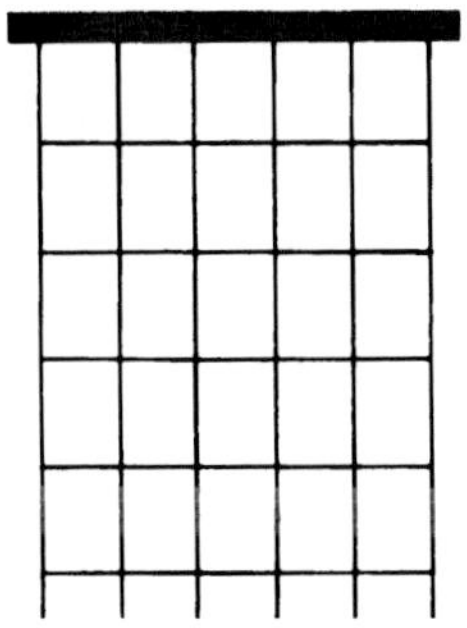
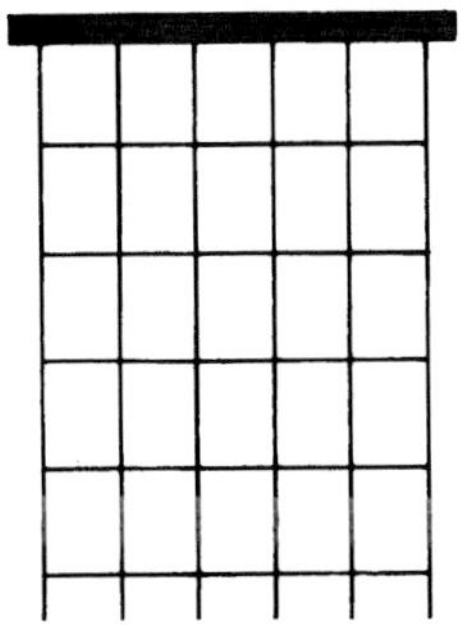
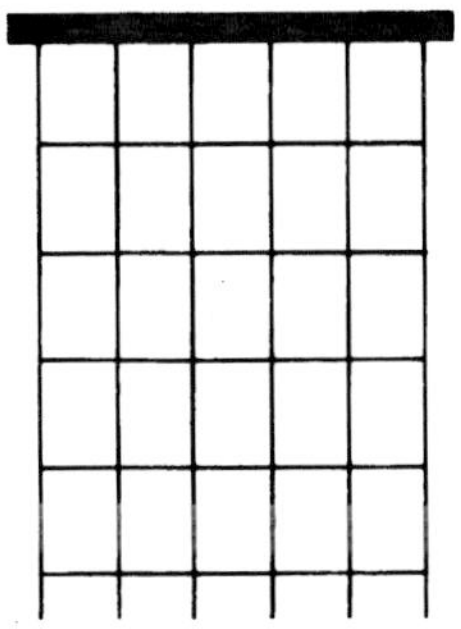
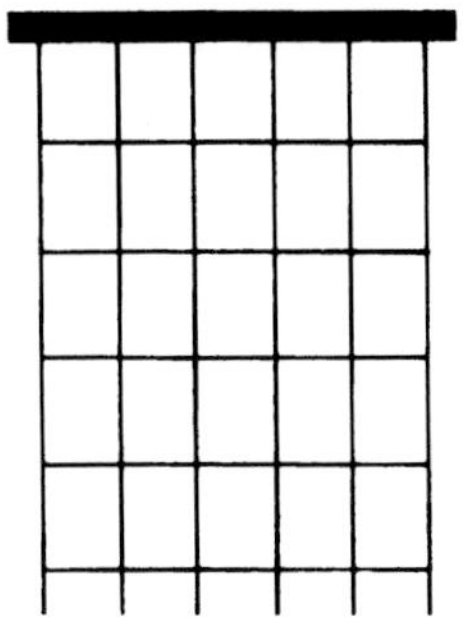
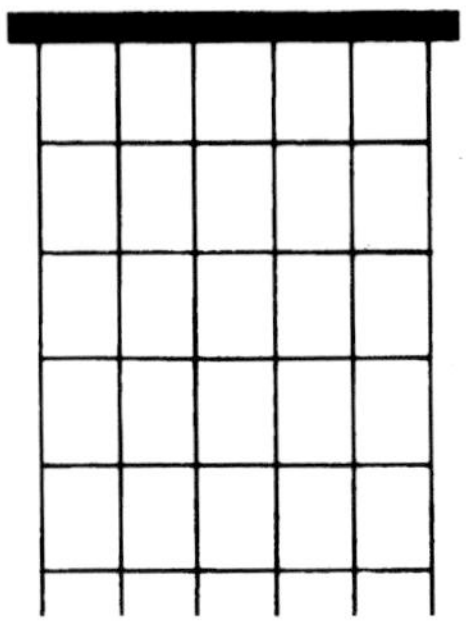
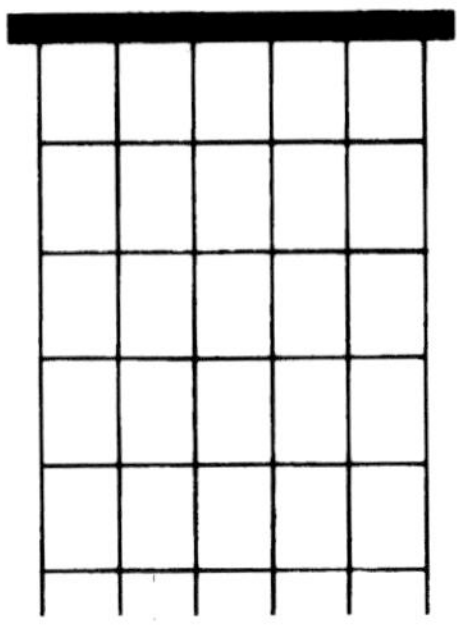
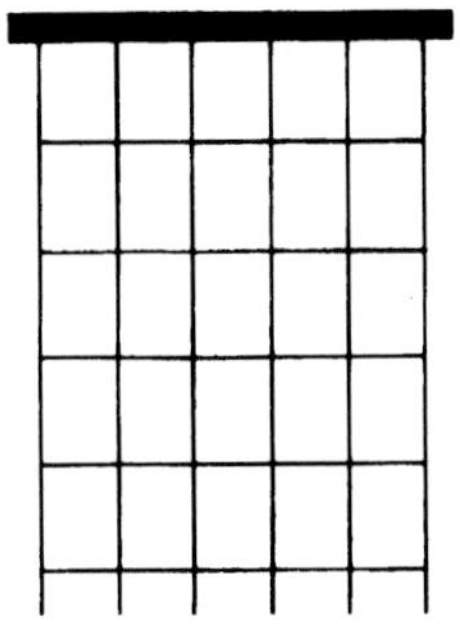
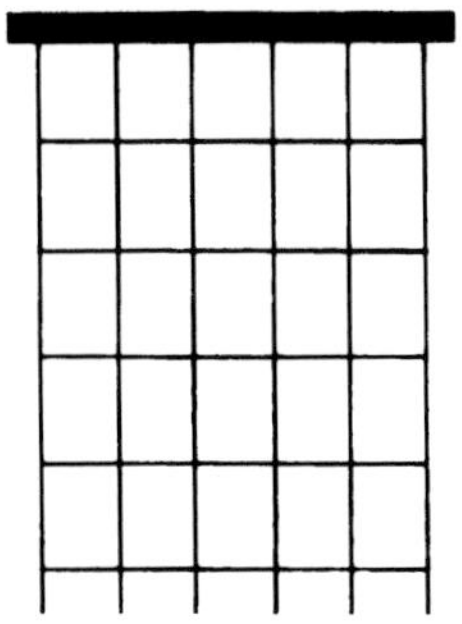
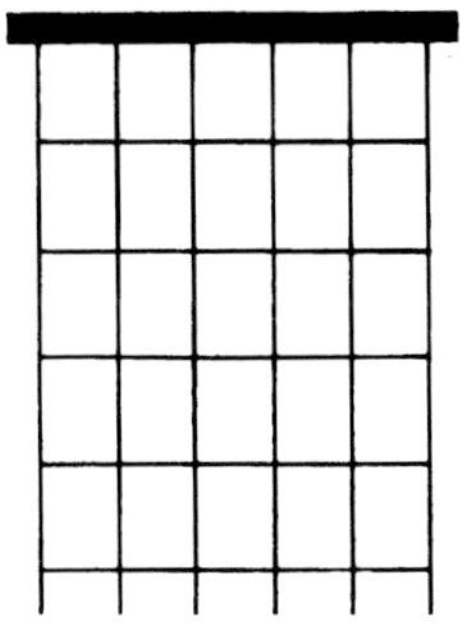
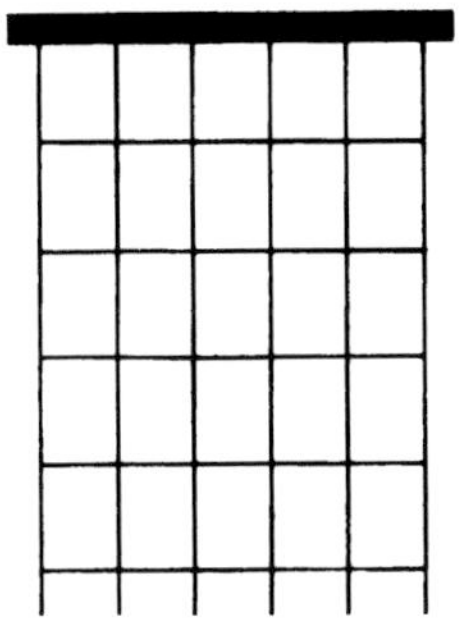
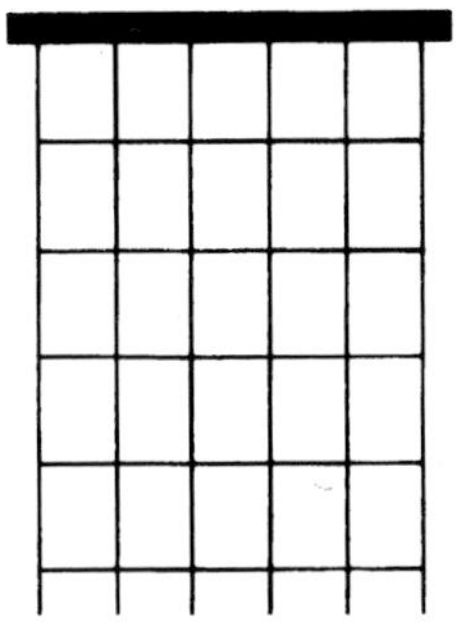
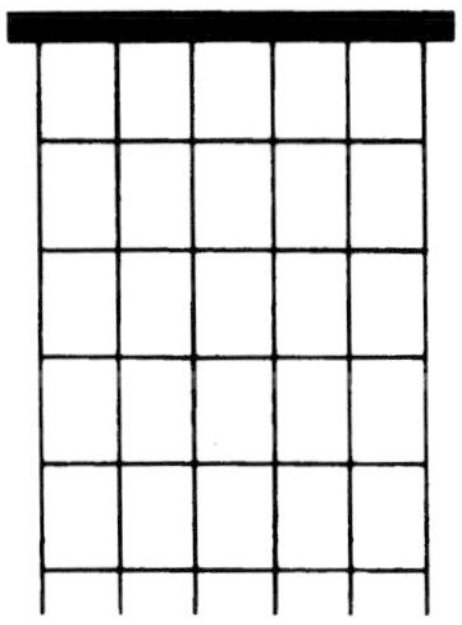
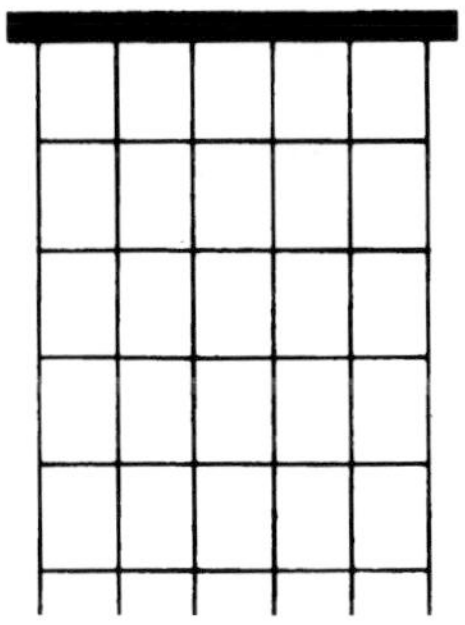
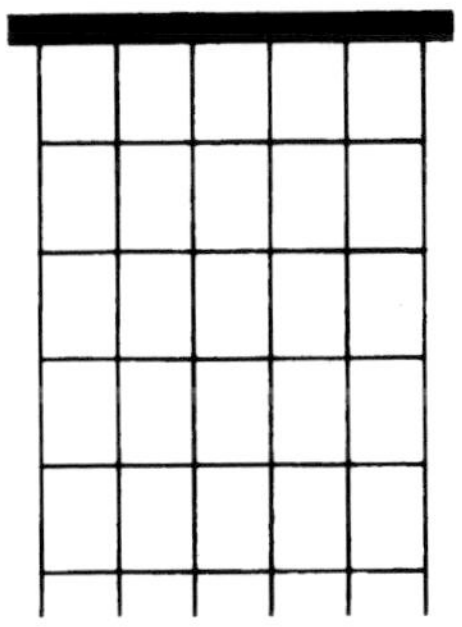
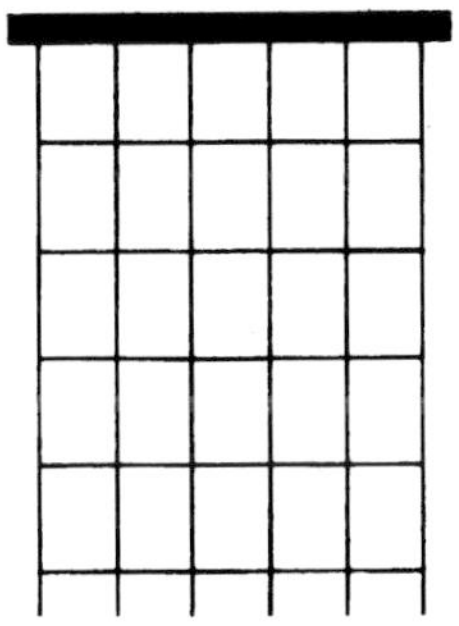
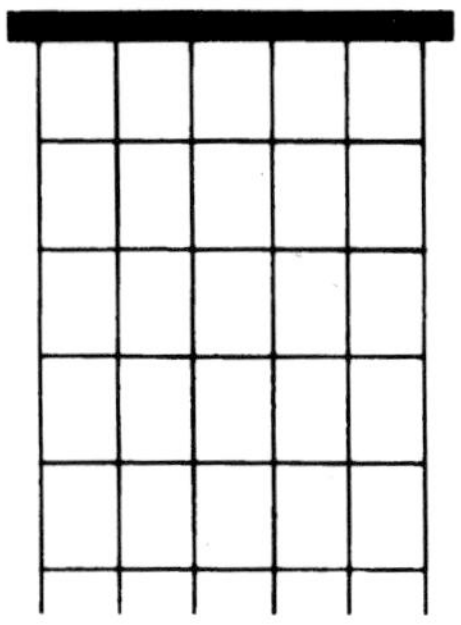
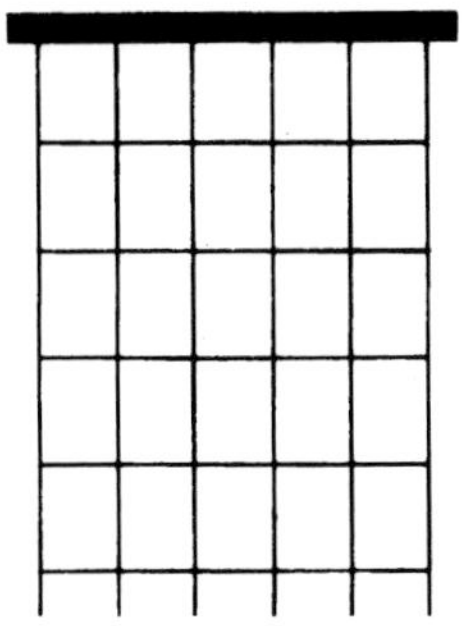
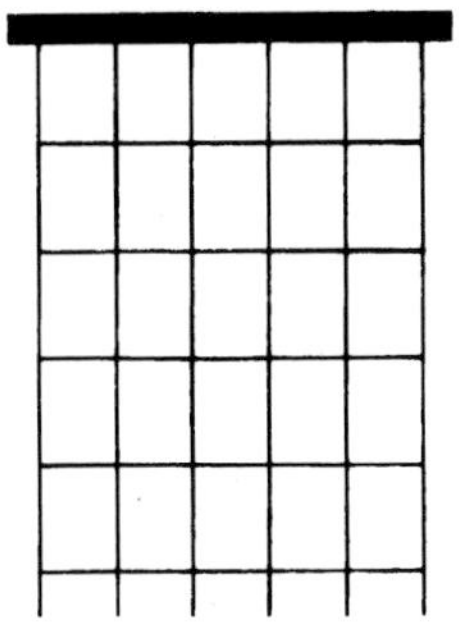
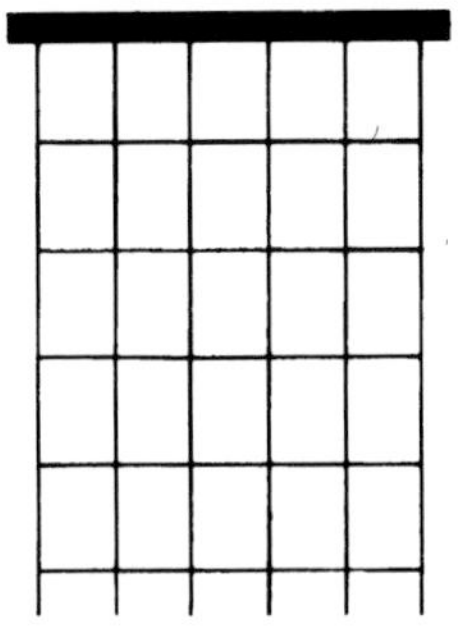

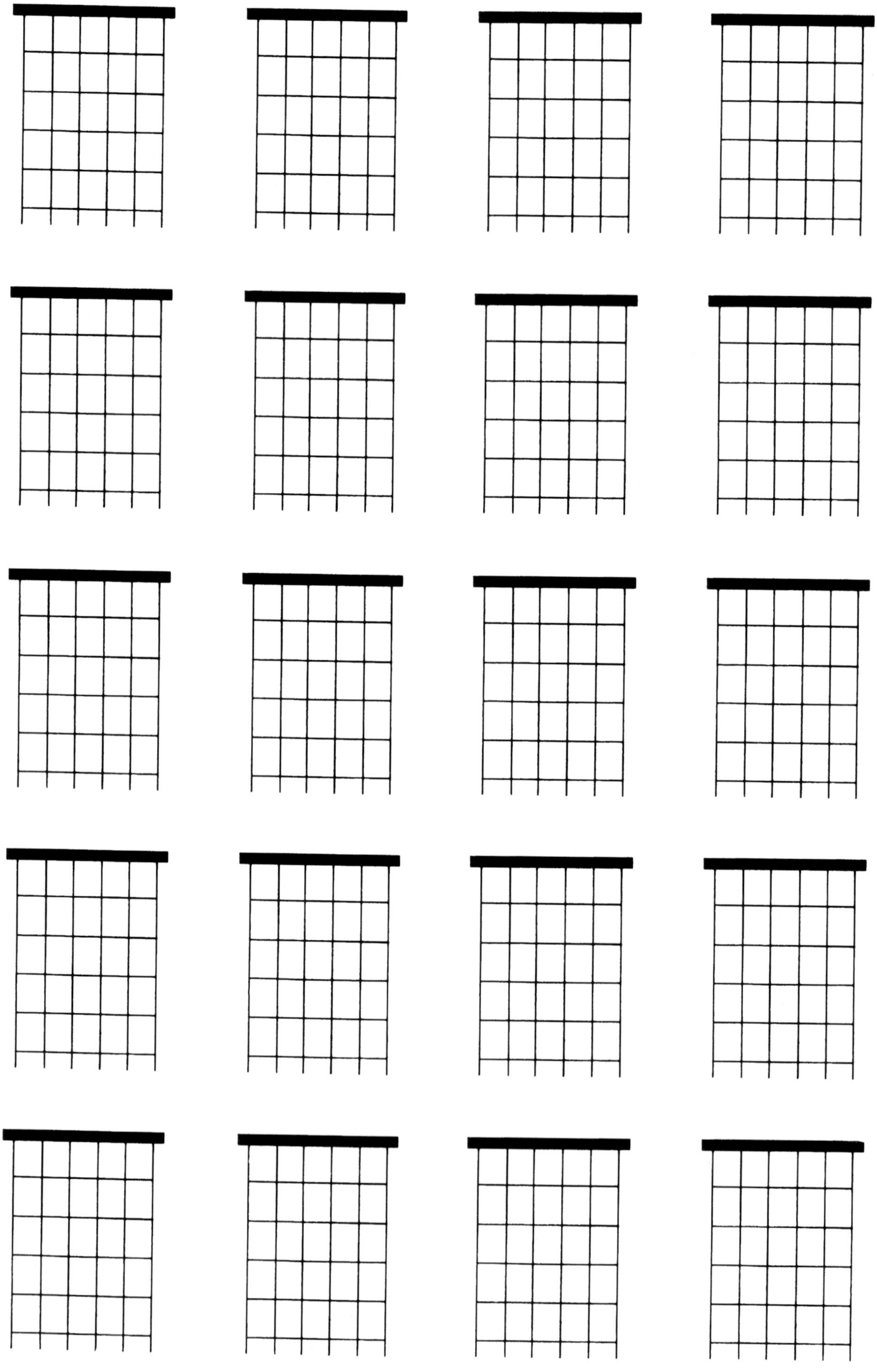

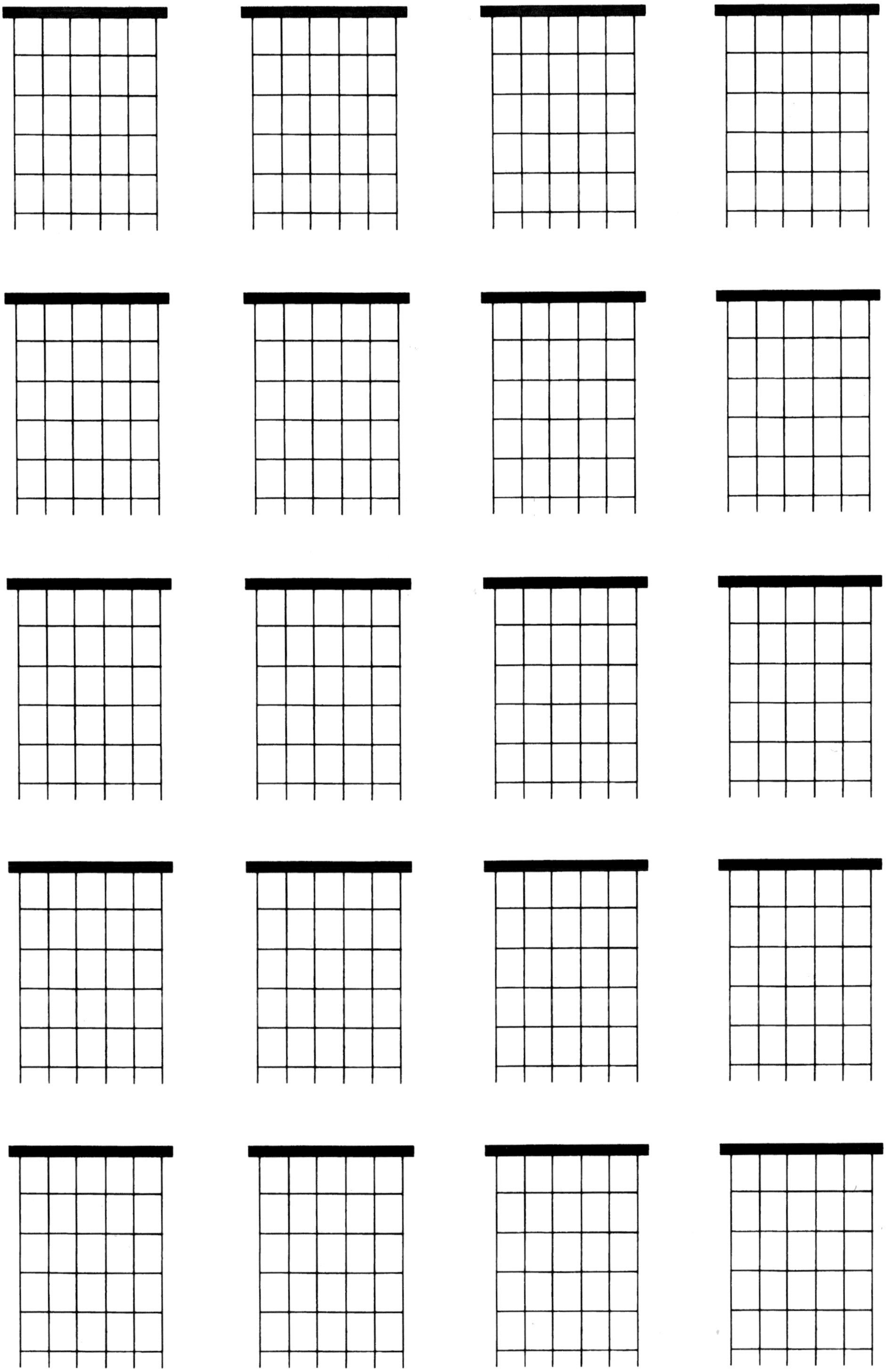

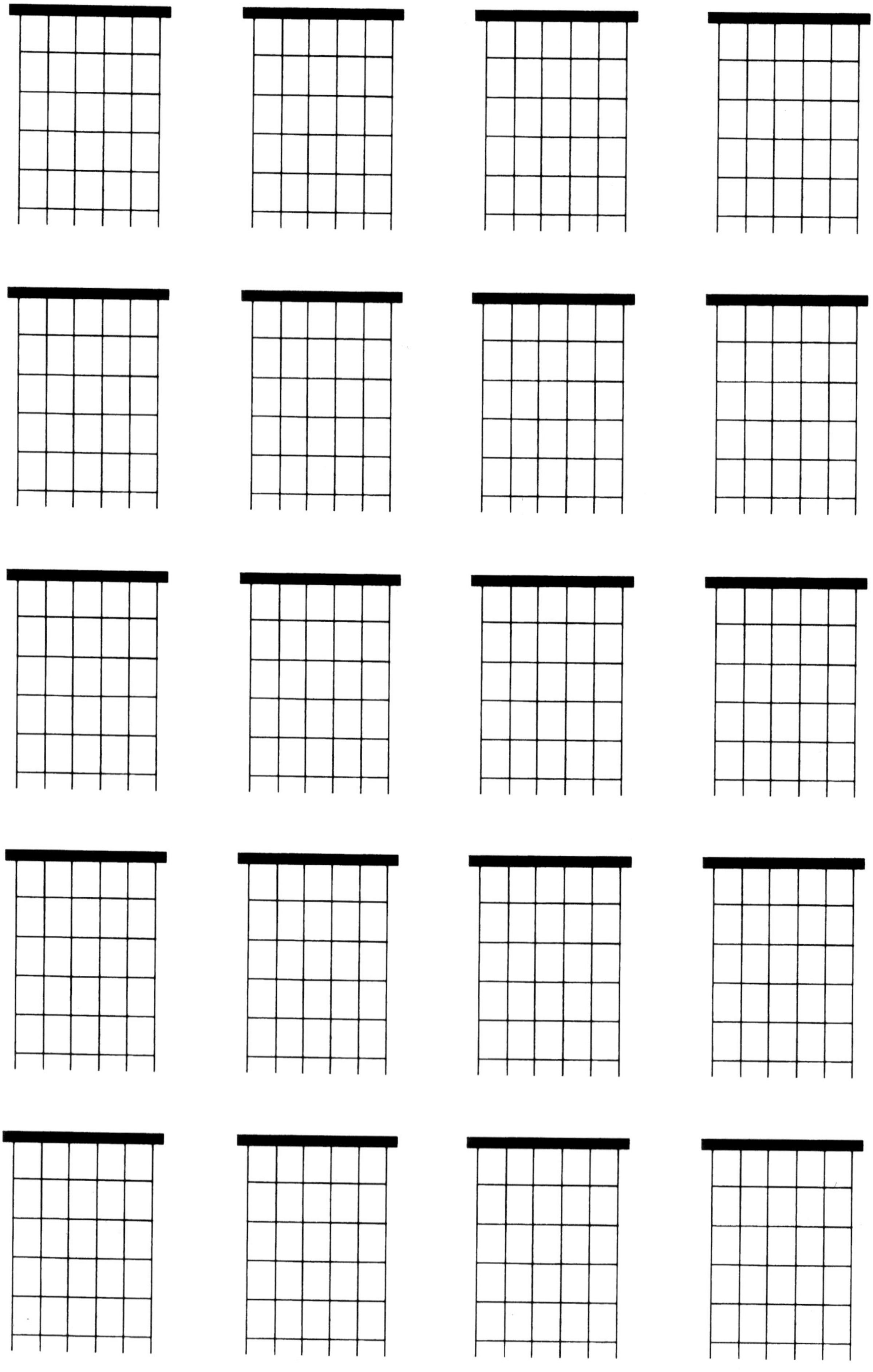

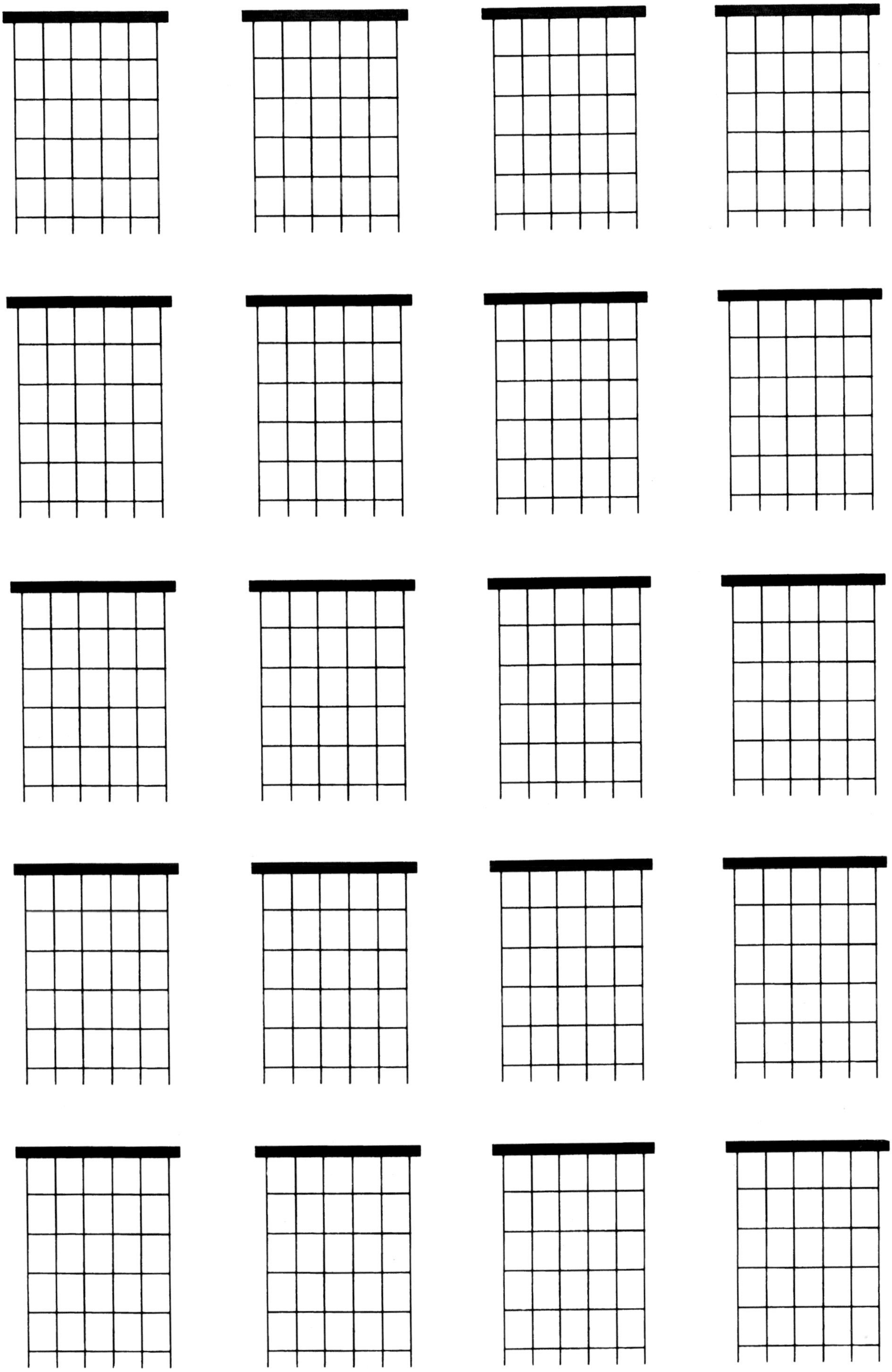

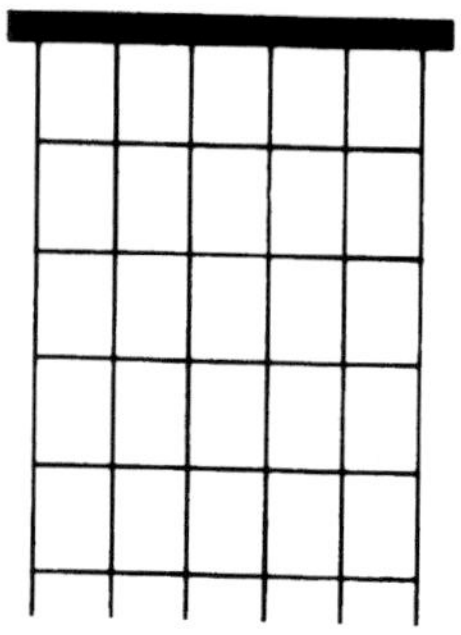
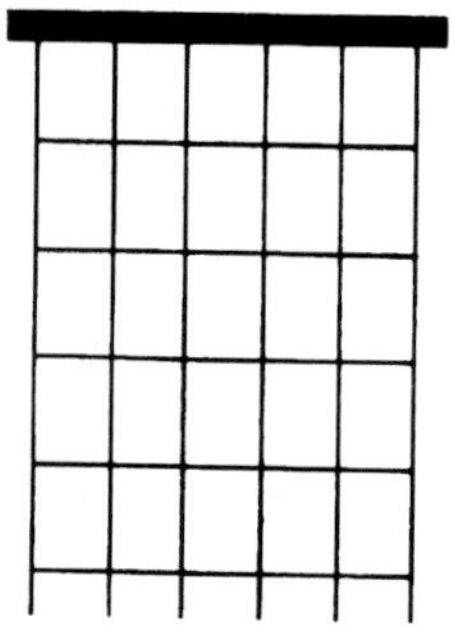
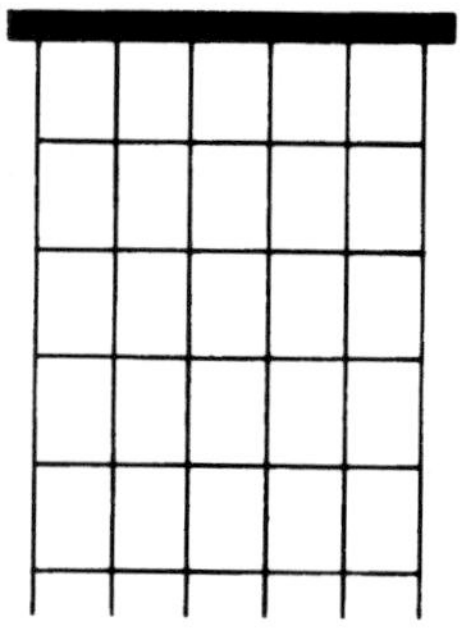
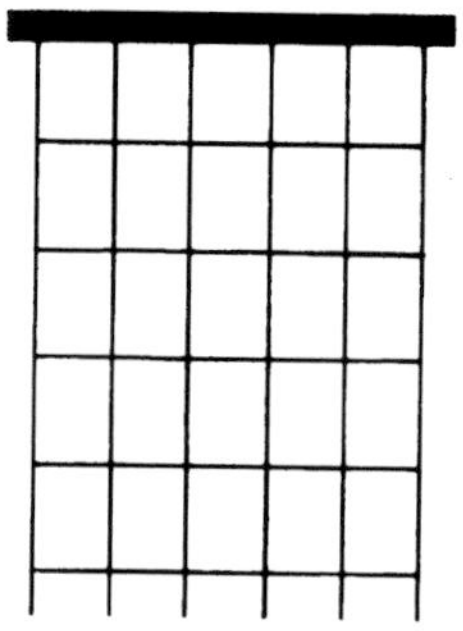
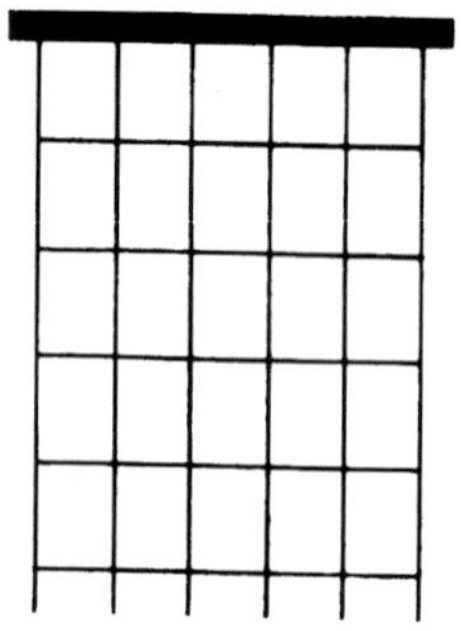
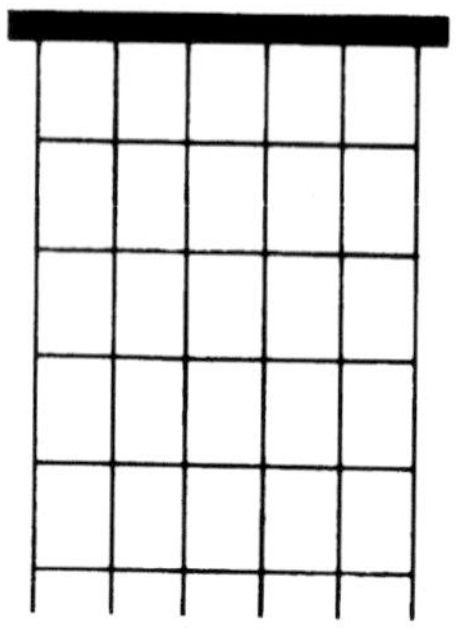
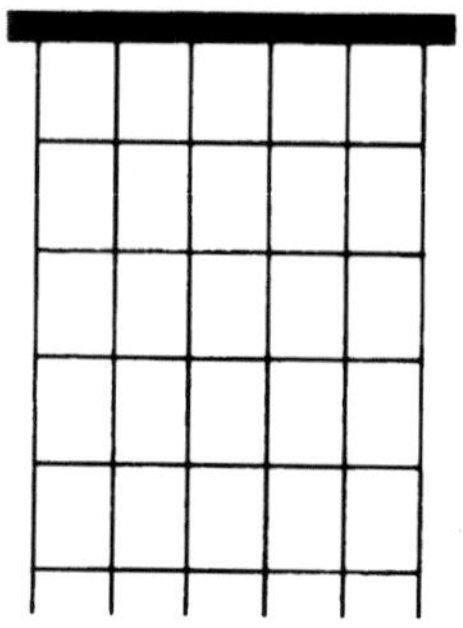
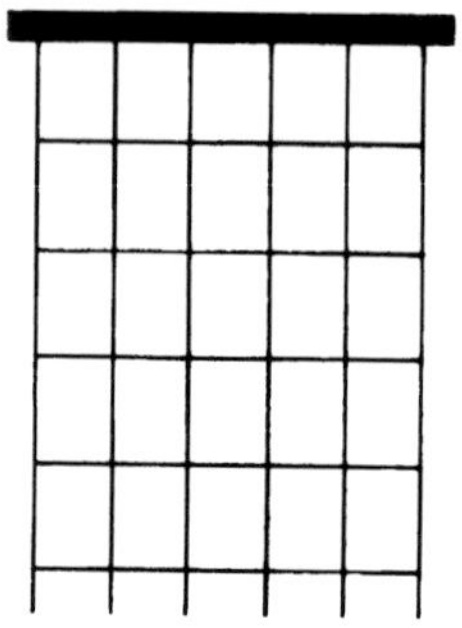
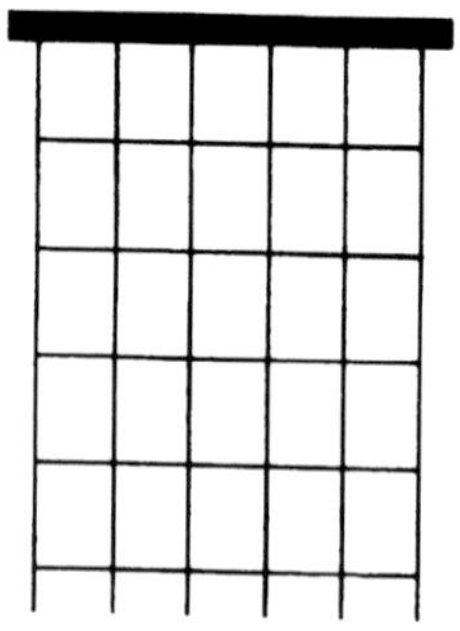
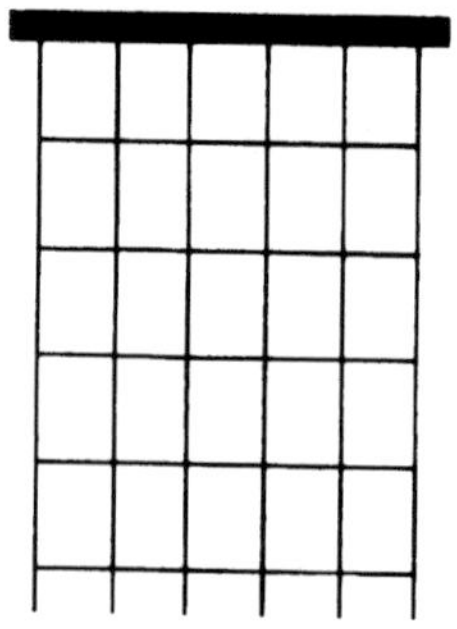
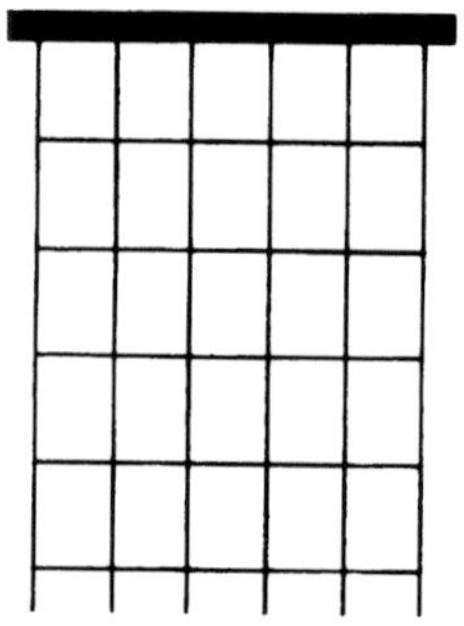
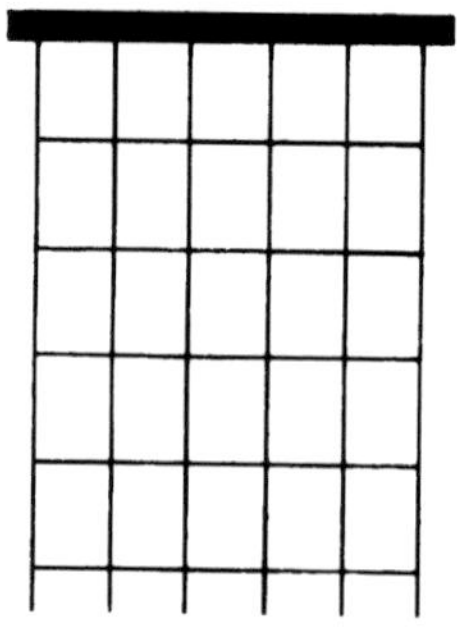
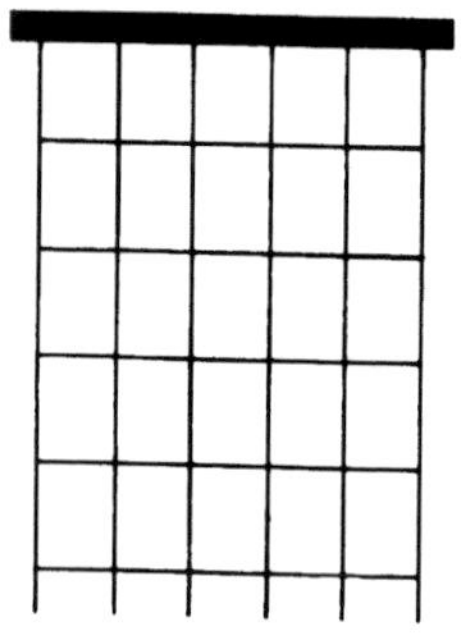
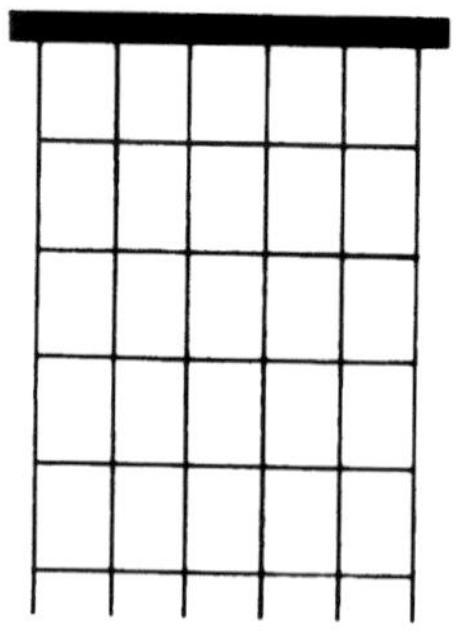
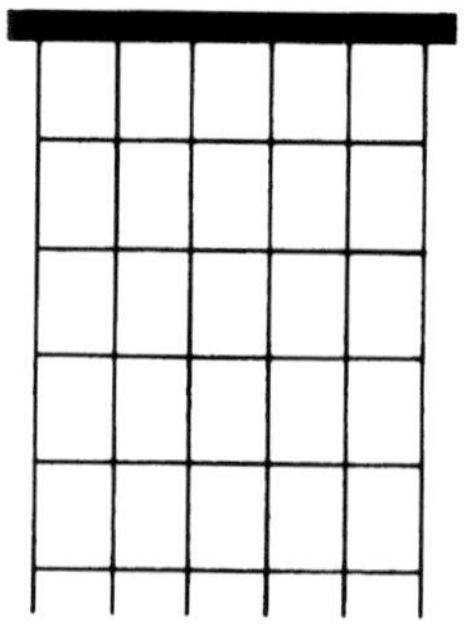
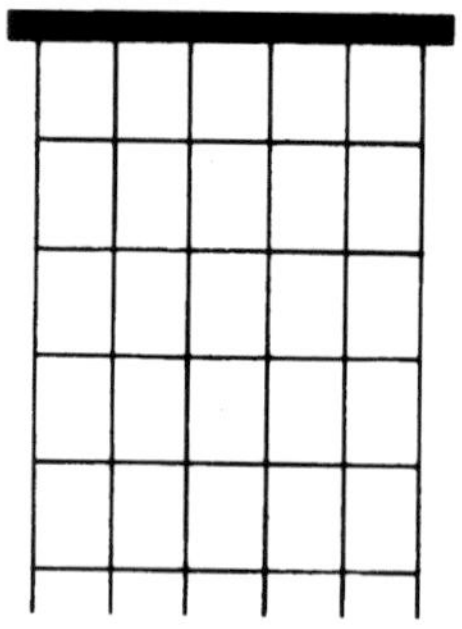
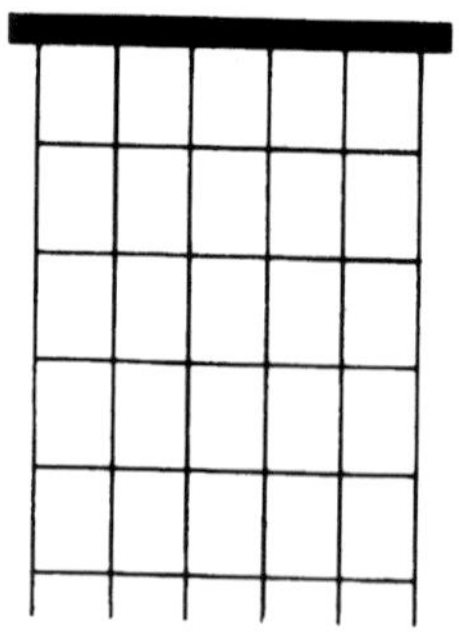
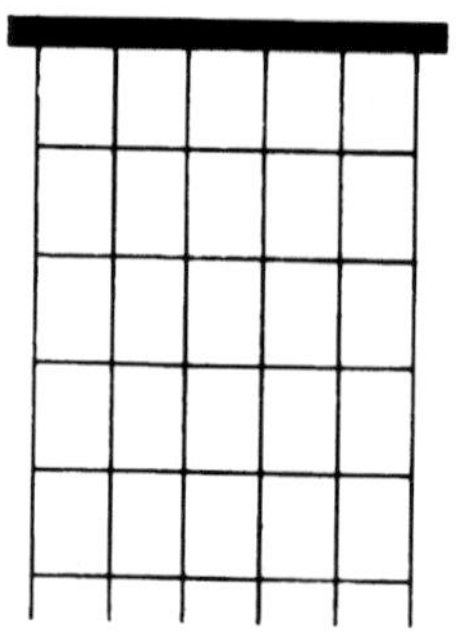
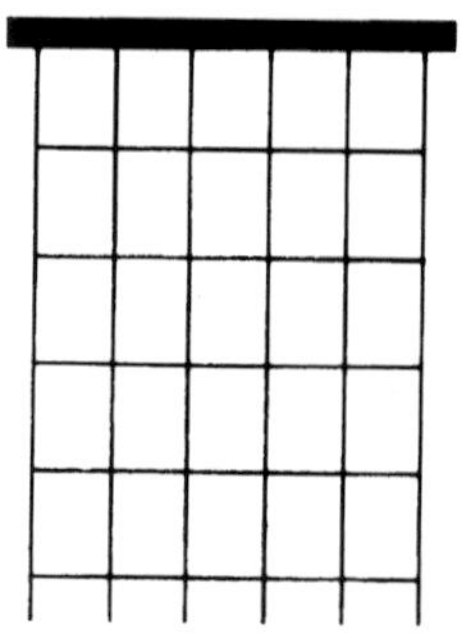
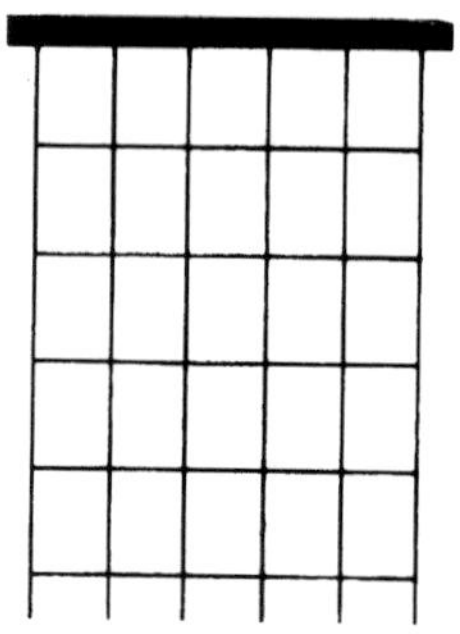

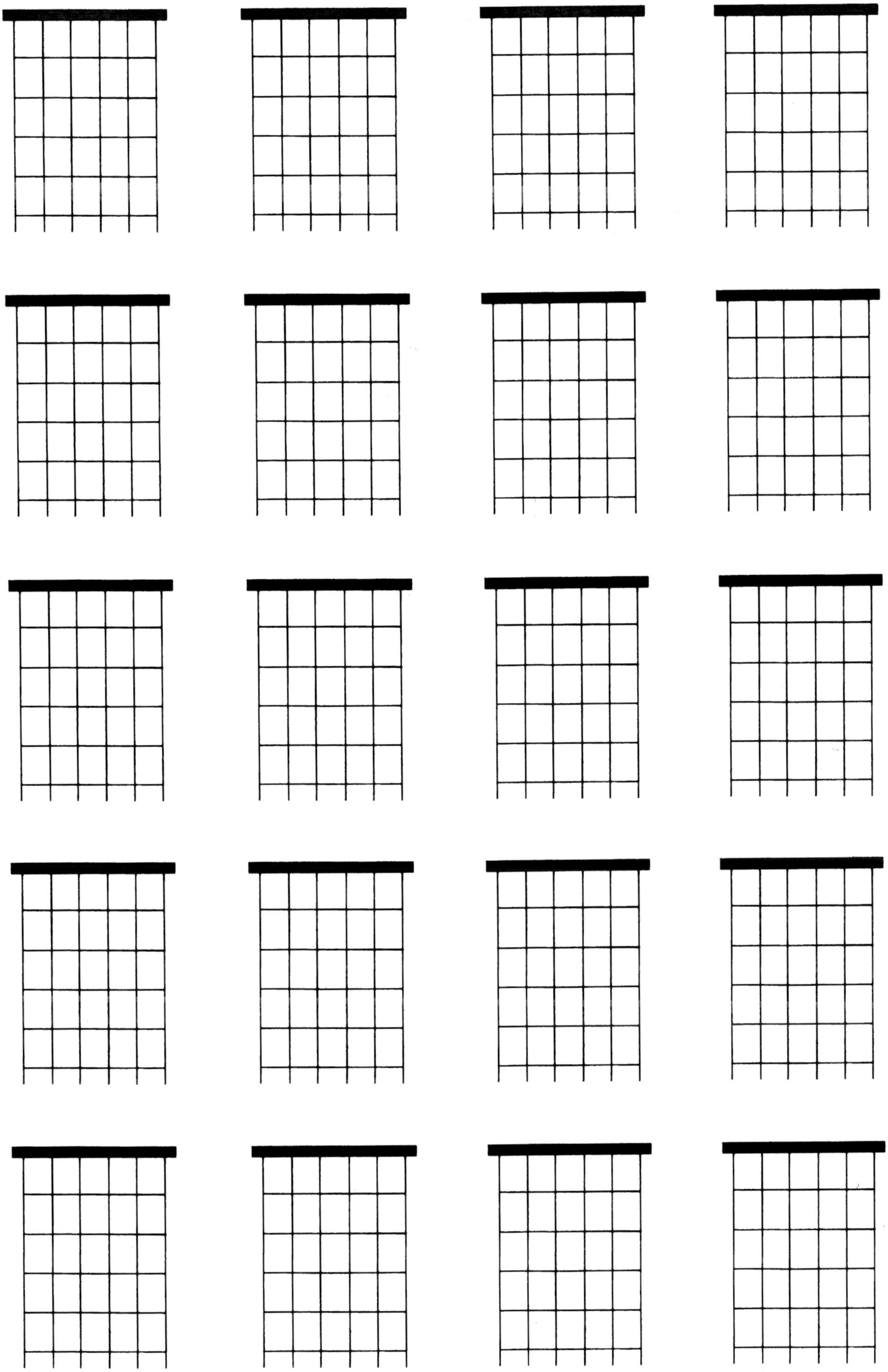

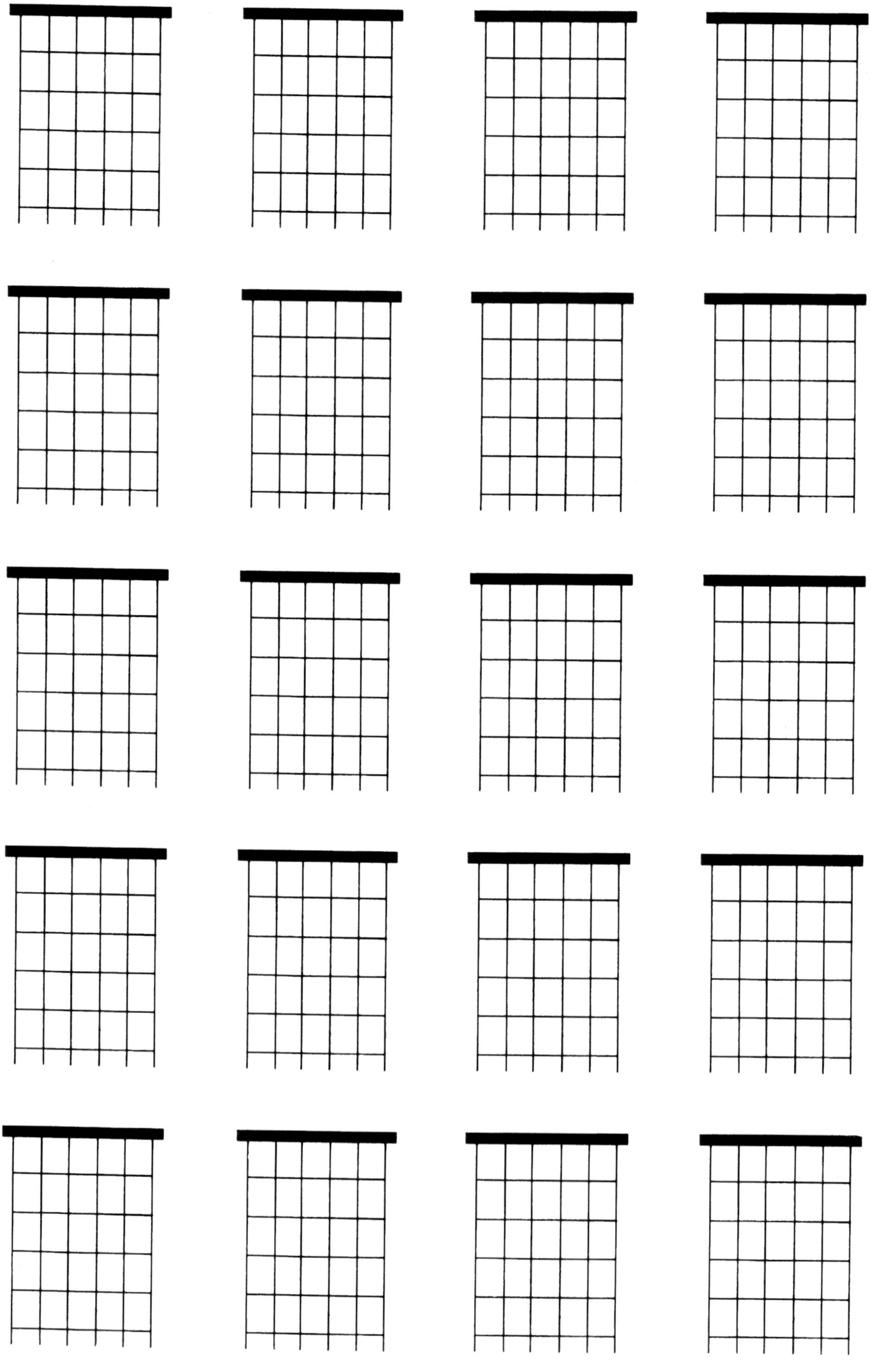

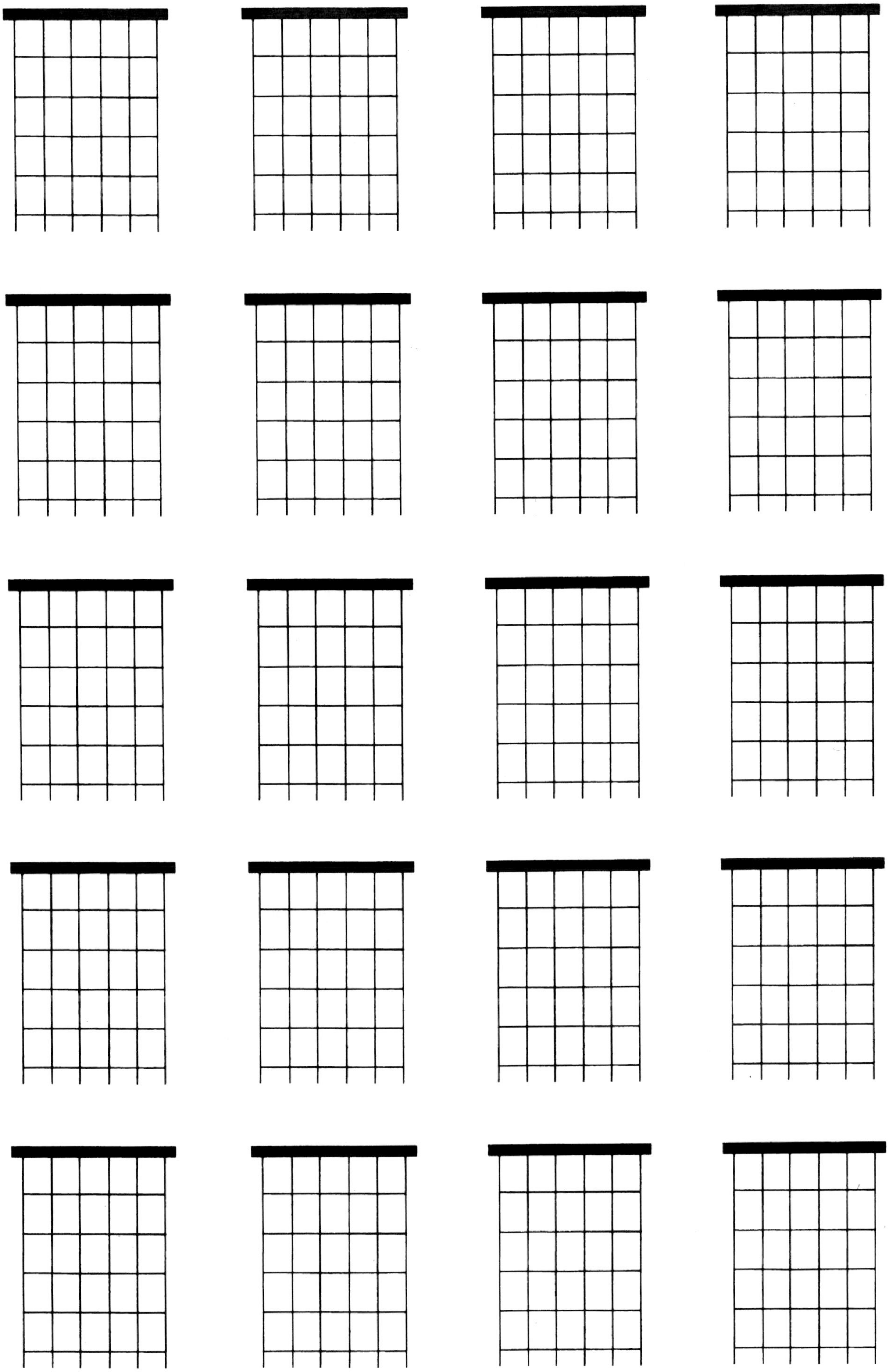

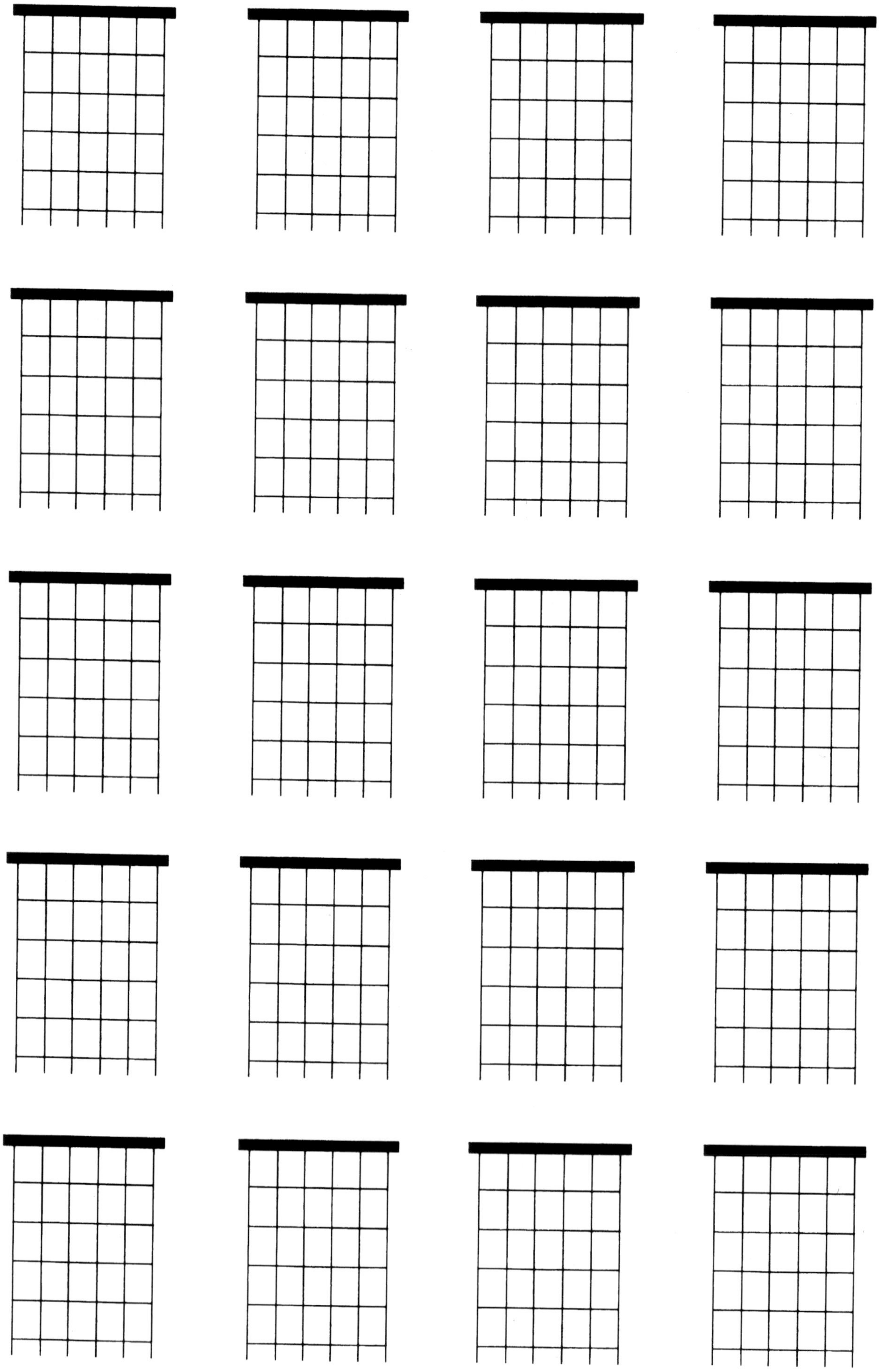

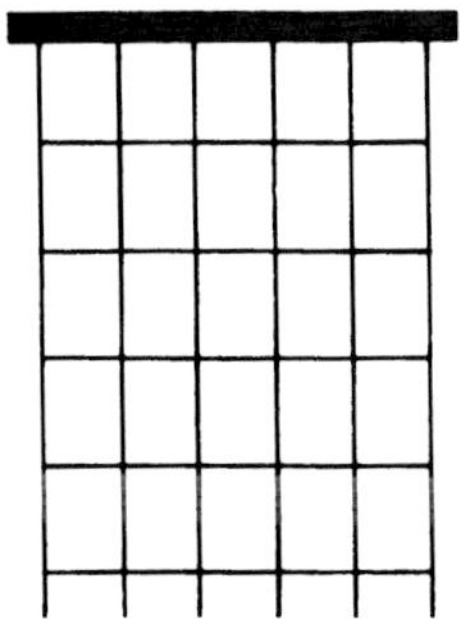
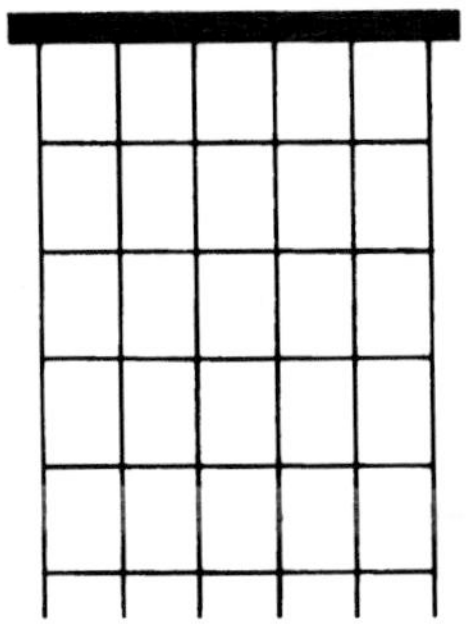
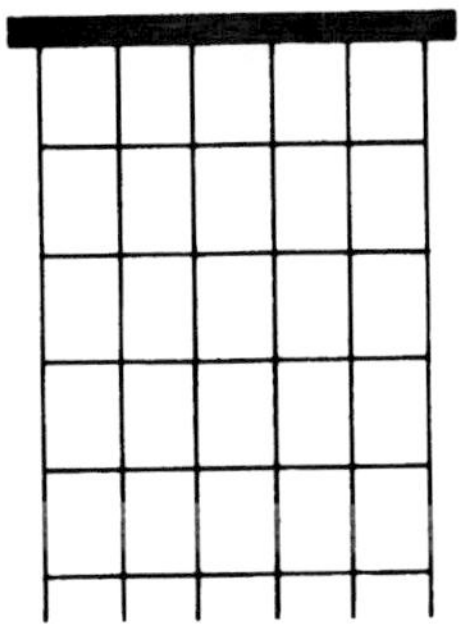
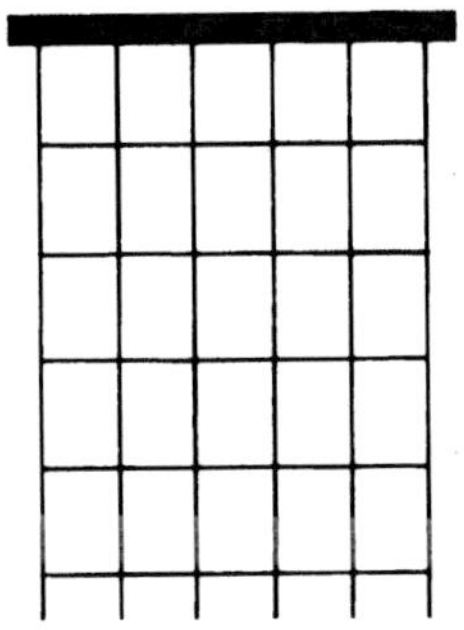
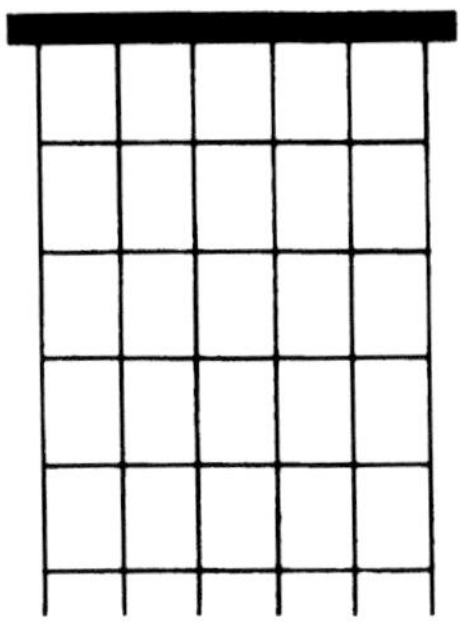
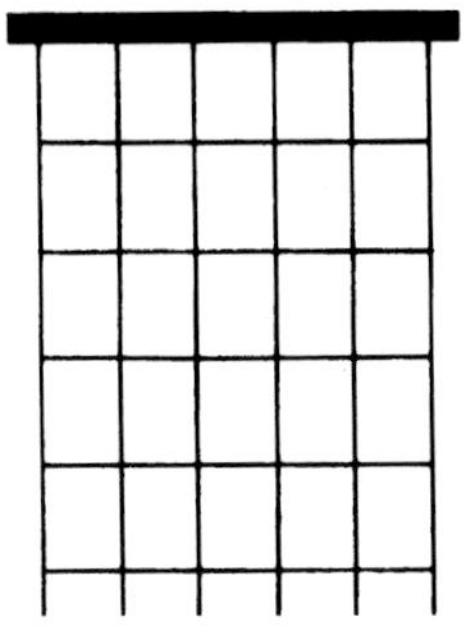
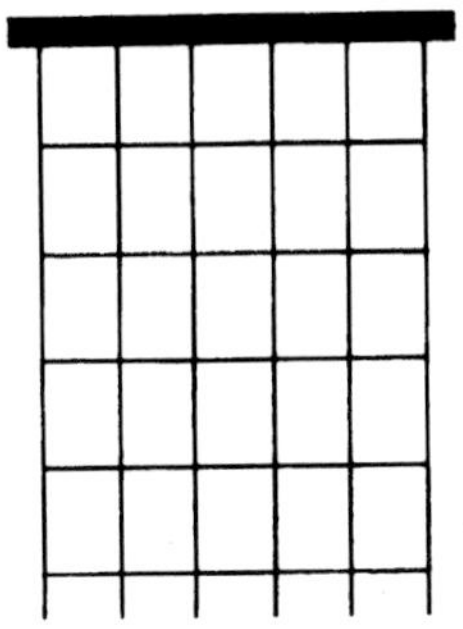
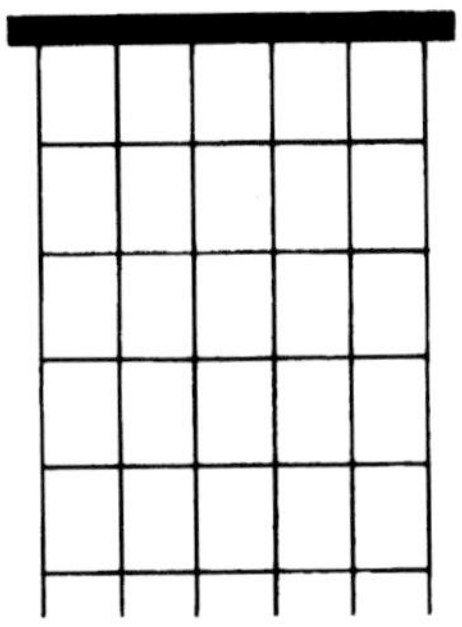
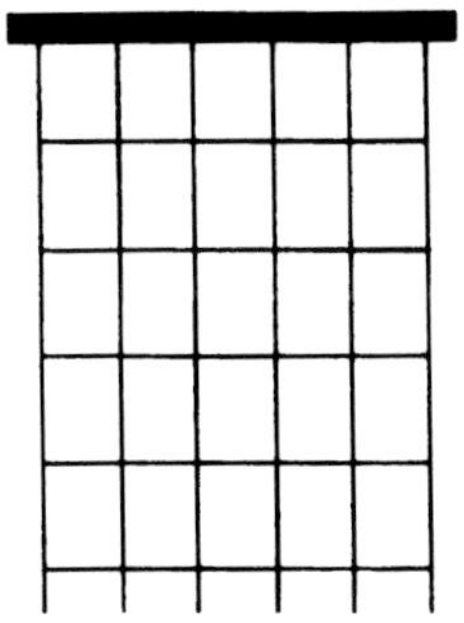
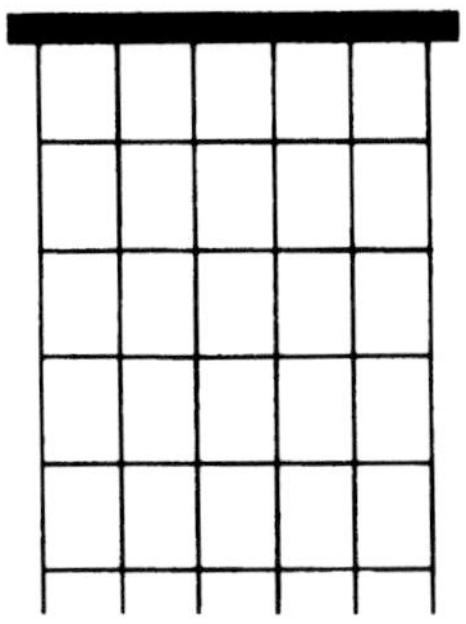
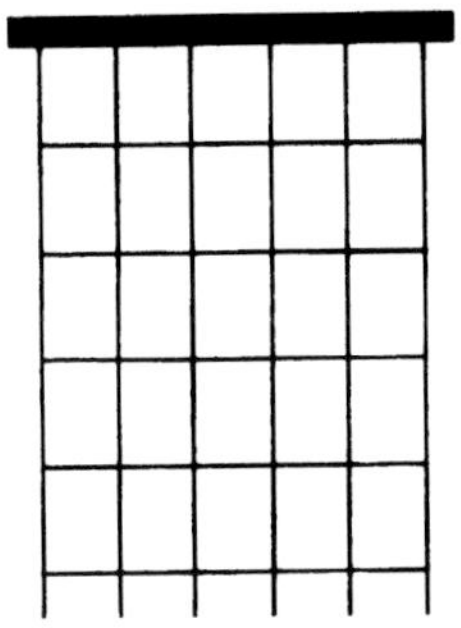
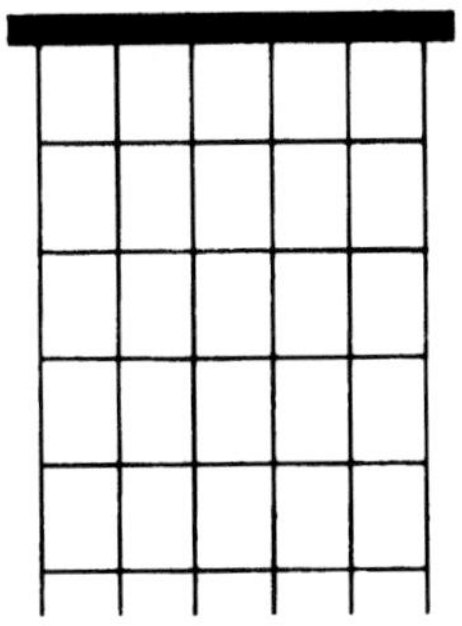
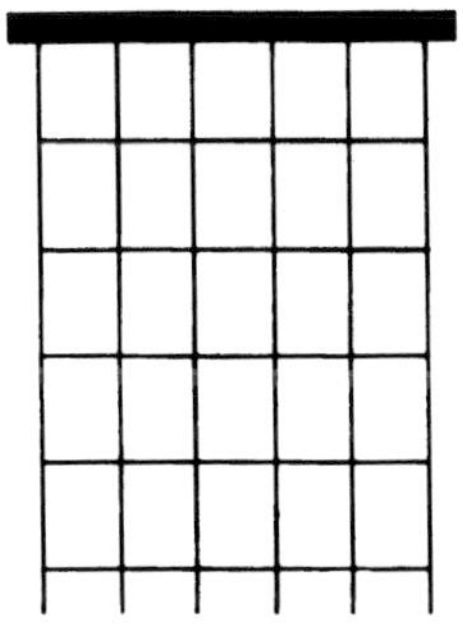
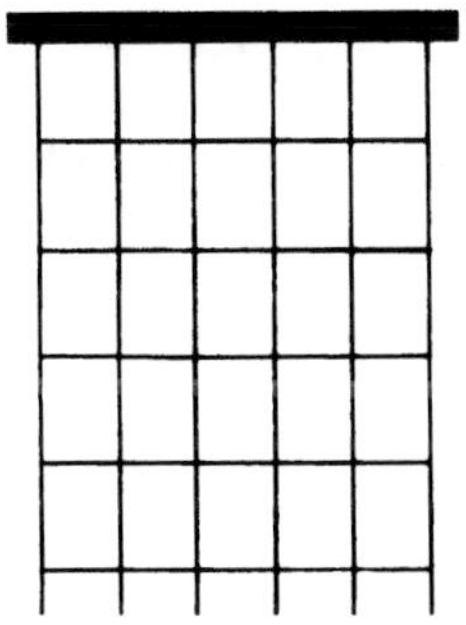
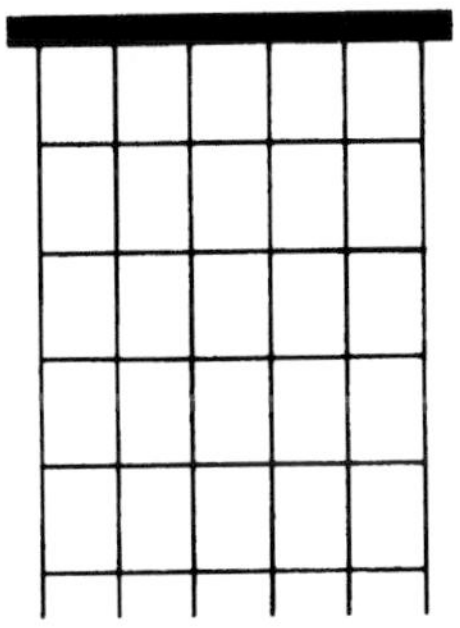
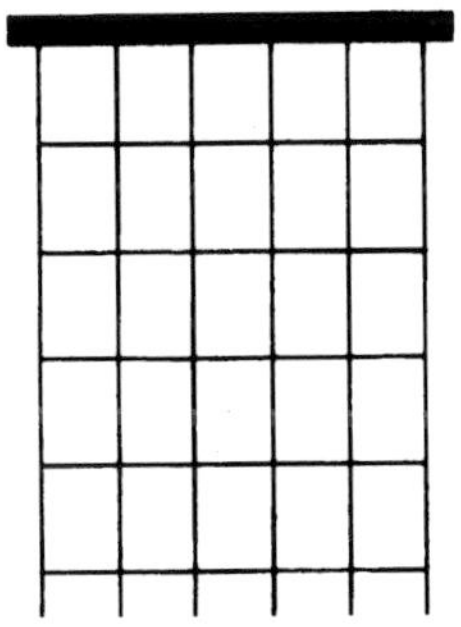
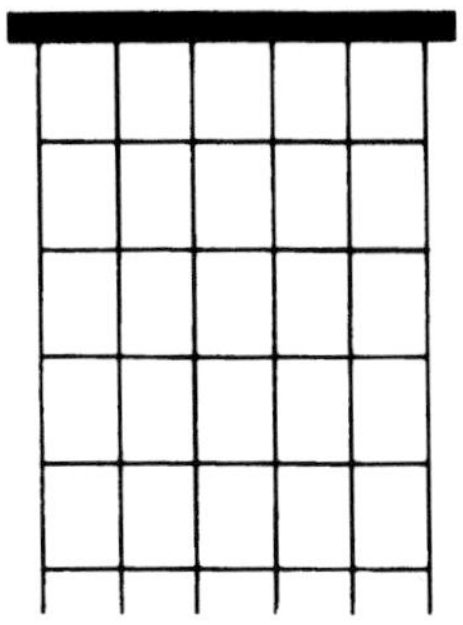
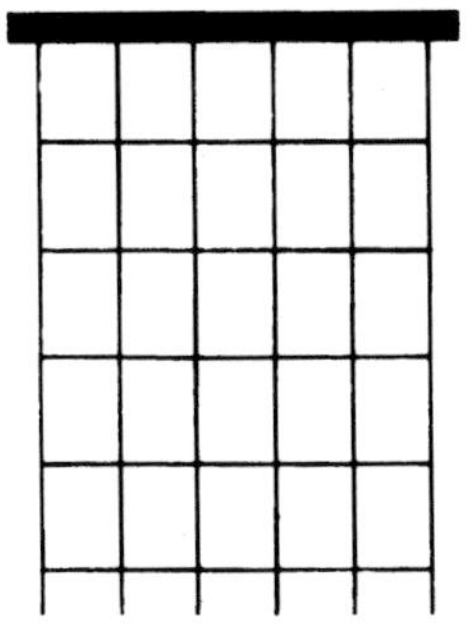
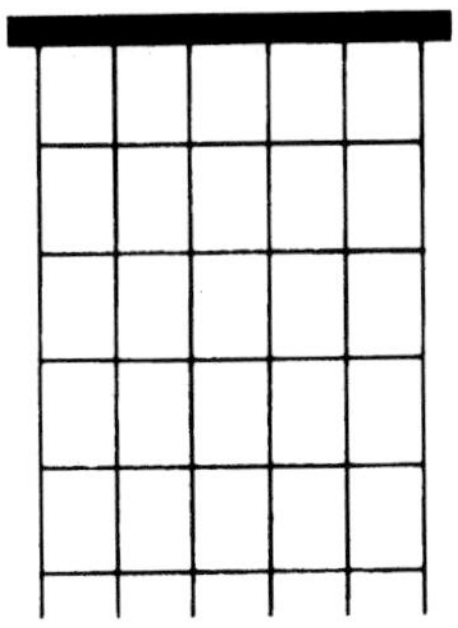
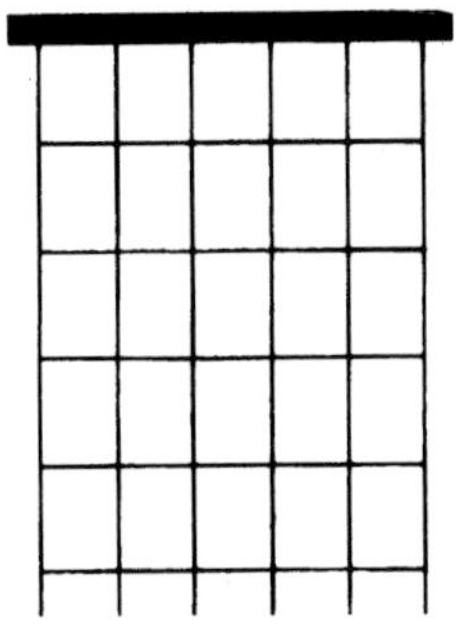

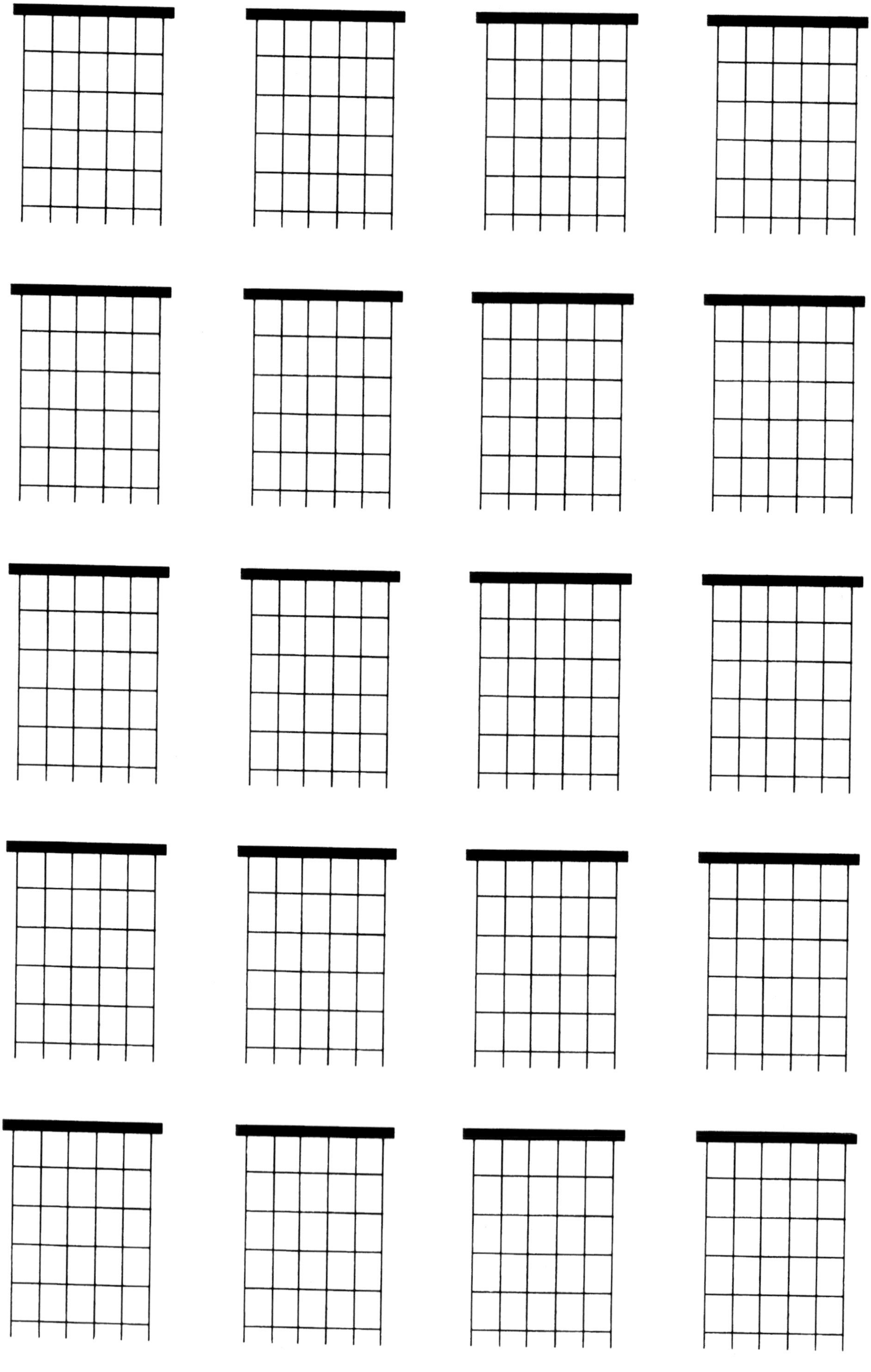

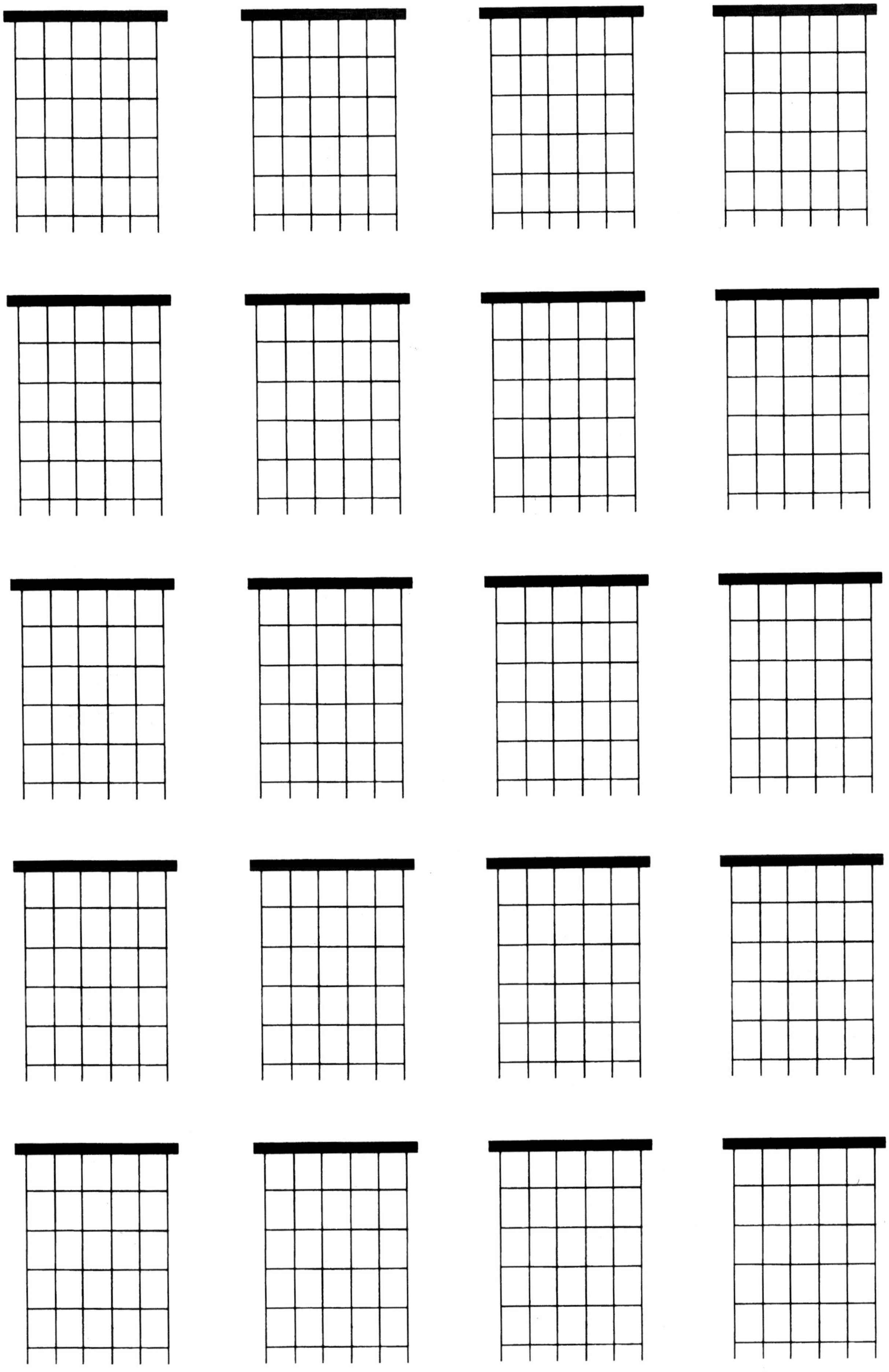

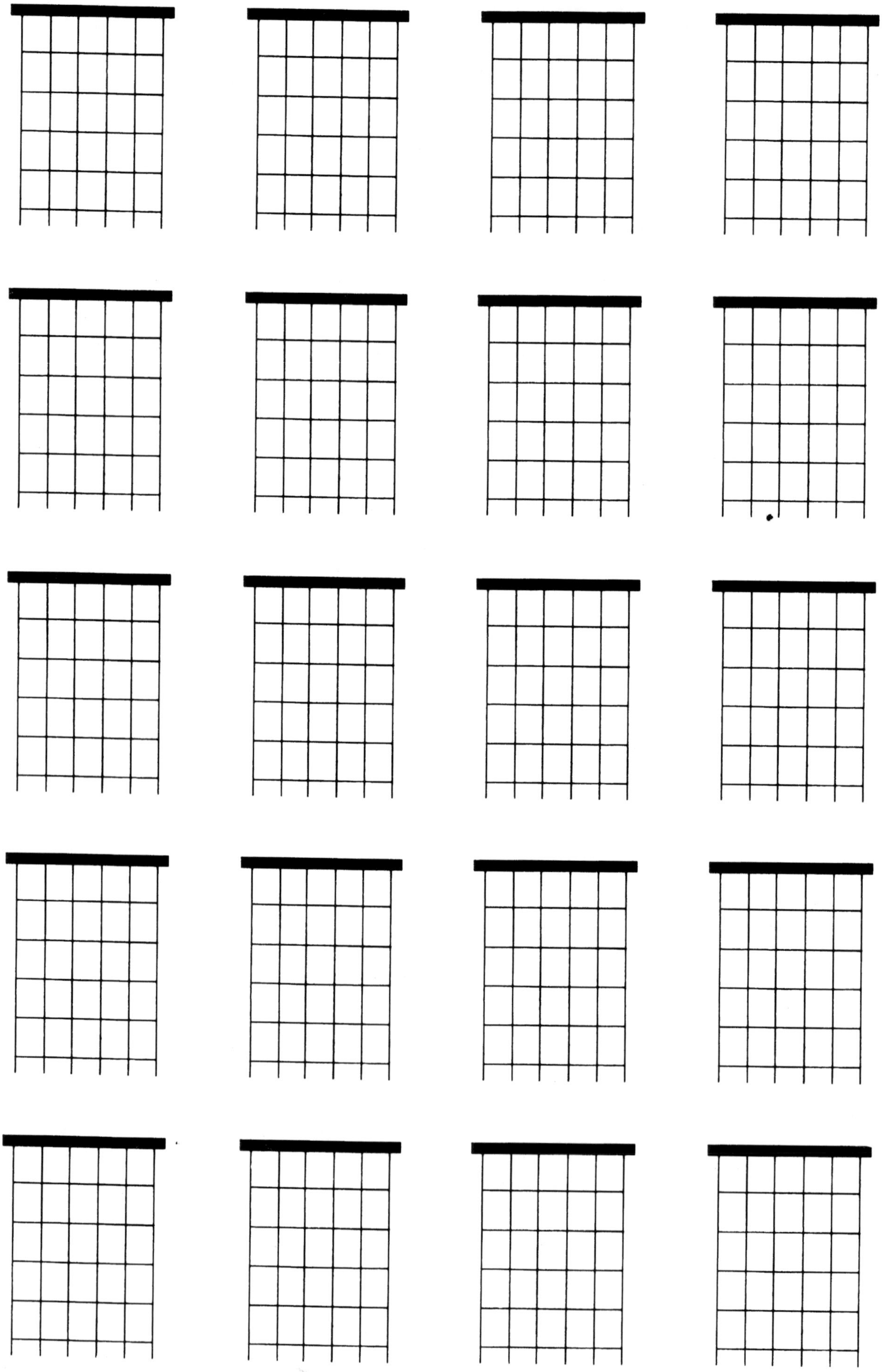